Corporate Directorship Practices:

Compensation 1975

By Jeremy Bacon

A Joint Research Report from The Conference Board
and the American Society of Corporate Secretaries, Inc.

Contents

Tables

Charts

Foreword

THIS VOLUME PROVIDES INFORMATION on the compensation of directors by 987 United States business firms. It focuses on fees and retainers for regular board service and for service on board committees, but also covers fringe benefits, reimbursement of travel and other meeting expenses, and the use of directors' and officers' liability insurance to provide protection to board members. The data and practices are those in effect in 1975.

This report updates one with the same title that was based on 1972 data and was published in 1973. We contemplate that a new edition, containing compensation and related information for that year, will be issued toward the end of every odd-numbered calendar year.

This report is part of a continuing series on corporate directorship practices undertaken jointly by the American Society of Corporate Secretaries, Inc. and THE CONFERENCE BOARD. Both organizations have been involved in planning and financing these studies. For this one, the Society, as in the past, has enlisted the cooperation of its members, who make up the great majority of the participants. The Board has processed and analyzed the data and prepared the text, tables and charts. The persons chiefly responsible for this fruitful collaboration of our two organizations are John S. Black, Jr. and Haworth White, Executive Director and Assistant Executive Director of the Society; and James K. Brown, Director, and Jeremy Bacon, Senior Research Associate, of the Board's Management Planning and Systems Research unit.

We offer thanks to all those executives who completed lengthy questionnaires about their companies' directors' compensation. We are especially pleased to note that the number of respondents exceeded that for the 1973 study by almost 20 percent.

ALEXANDER B. TROWBRIDGE
President
The Conference Board

JOHN C. CARTER
President
American Society of Corporate Secretaries, Inc.

About This Report and How to Use It

The following information should be helpful to the reader in interpreting this report:

Respondents: Although most of the companies included in this study also participated in the 1973 edition (which was based on 1972 data), the samples are not identical. (There are 987 companies represented in this compensation study, compared with 833 in the earlier edition, an increase of almost 20 percent. Of the 987, 570 are manufacturing and 417 are nonmanufacturing companies.) Like its predecessors, this report covers only U.S. corporations.

Presentation of material: Data on compensation for regular board service is presented separately for manufacturing and for nonmanufacturing companies, to reflect apparent differences. As a rule, this distinction is not maintained for other material (committee compensation, fringe benefits, meeting expense reimbursement, and so on).

One change from the 1973 report is the inclusion, in Tables 3 and 5 (showing the compensation practices of individual companies) of codes indicating company size in terms of assets. This addition should facilitate comparisons for readers interested in learning how much other firms in their industry "about the same size as mine" pay their directors.

Throughout this report, the term "retainer" indicates an amount paid on an annual basis (although it may be actually paid out in installments during the year) that is not related to and does not depend on attendance at board (or committee) meetings. The term "fee" indicates an amount paid for attendance on a per-meeting basis.

As in the 1973 report, figures are given for annual compensation of directors, taking into account both per-meeting fees and annual retainers. The annualized fee amount in each case presumes attendance at all regularly scheduled meetings of the board, as reported by each company. A director who fails to attend all such meetings in a year would ordinarily receive less than this amount, whereas he would receive a greater amount if he were to attend special meetings of the board in addition to those regularly scheduled.

Percentages and medians: In each case, the total number of companies on which a percentage is based equals the number answering the particular question or part of a question; companies that did not reply or indicated that the question was not applicable are omitted from the calculation and from the number of reporting companies shown in the table heading.

Medians rather than mathematical averages are used to show representative or typical values. (A median is the middle value in a distribution, above and below which lie an equal number of values.) In those few cases in which the median falls between two whole numbers, it has been computed.

Basic Findings

- Almost every company pays outside directors for board service. Most companies do not pay directors' compensation as such to employees who serve on the board. (Pages 2, 32, 54.)
- Amounts of compensation to outside directors in 1975 show substantial increases over 1972 figures. Median annual compensation figures for regular board service have increased in almost every industry, by increments of from about 10 percent to as high as more than 100 percent, but mostly in the range of 15 to 40 percent. (Pages 2, 32.)
- The annual retainer has continued to gain favor as a form of compensation to outside directors. A majority (slightly more than 60 percent) of companies in the report pay *both* a retainer and a per-meeting attendance fee. (Pages 2, 32.)
- Compensation of outside directors in manufacturing companies is significantly higher, on the average, than that of directors of nonmanufacturing companies. In particular, banks and utilities, both well represented in this report, pay their directors less than do manufacturing companies of comparable asset size. (Pages 3-6, 33 and 34.)
- For manufacturing companies, there is a consistent correlation between size and outside directors' compensation, with large companies paying more on the average. The extremes in the range: Median annual compensation for the smallest manufacturing companies (assets of under $10 million), $800; for the largest companies, with $3 billion in assets, $13,000. (Chart 2, page 4.) The relationship between company size and directors' compensation is less uniform among nonmanufacturing companies. (Chart 6, page 33.)
- More than three-quarters of respondents pay outside directors (few pay employee directors) for service on some or all committees of the board. About a fifth of the reporting firms pay committee chairmen more—sometimes substantially more—than other committee members. (Pages 56-59.)
- Most companies offer directors protection, by means of indemnification agreements, from financial loss stemming from their liability as directors; a majority provide supplemental protection in the form of "directors' and officers' liability insurance." (Page 69.)

1. Compensation of Outside Directors for Regular Board Service

THIS SECTION PRESENTS INFORMATION on compensation of outside directors for regular board service; compensation for committee service is dealt with in Section 3, beginning on page 58. Because compensation for regular board service in manufacturing companies tends to differ somewhat in form and amount from that in nonmanufacturing companies, the information for the two types of industries is presented separately.

Manufacturing Companies

All but seven manufacturing companies (559 out of 566 responding) pay nonemployees for serving on the board of directors. The forms and amounts of such compensation are described below. (For definitions of *retainer* and *fee* as used in this report, see page vi.)

Forms of Compensation

As in 1972, a majority of manufacturing companies use both annual retainers and per-meeting fees to compensate their outside directors, as Table 1 shows.

Table 1: Forms of Compensation to Outside Directors in 559 Manufacturing Companies

Forms of Compensation	Percent of Companies Paying	
	1975	1972
Both retainer and fee	63%	60%
Retainer only	23	22
Fee only	14	18
	100%	100%

The figures in the table show that there has been a continuation of a trend toward greater use of the retainer as a means of compensating outside directors. This trend has also been evident in nonmanufacturing firms.

Amounts of Compensation

Charts 1 through 5 summarize information about how much manufacturing companies pay to outside directors. For data on individual companies, grouped by industry, see Table 3 beginning on page 8.

Increases in Compensation

Except for companies having assets of less than $50 million, annual compensation figures for outside directors of manufacturing companies in 1975 are considerably larger than the amounts reported in 1972. For example, the 1972

Chart 1: Annual Compensation of Outside Directors for Regular Board Service, 550 Manufacturing Companies, 406 Nonmanufacturing Companies

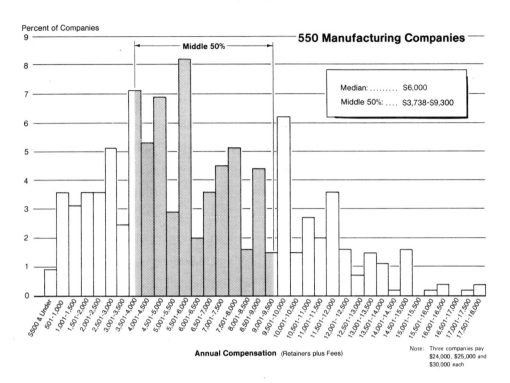

Percent of Companies

550 Manufacturing Companies

Middle 50%

| Median: | $6,000 |
| Middle 50%: | $3,738-$9,300 |

Annual Compensation (Retainers plus Fees)

Note: Three companies pay $24,000, $25,000 and $30,000 each

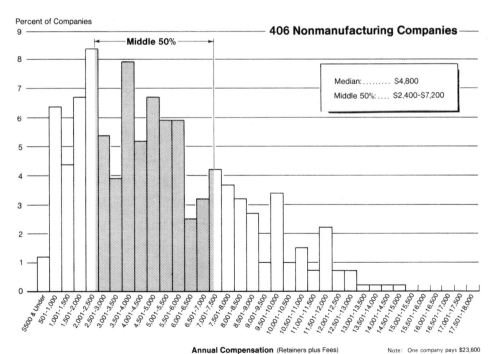

Percent of Companies

406 Nonmanufacturing Companies

Middle 50%

| Median: | $4,800 |
| Middle 50%: | $2,400-$7,200 |

Annual Compensation (Retainers plus Fees)

Note: One company pays $23,600

3

Chart 2: Annual Compensation of Outside Directors for Regular Board Service, by Company Size, 550 Manufacturing Companies

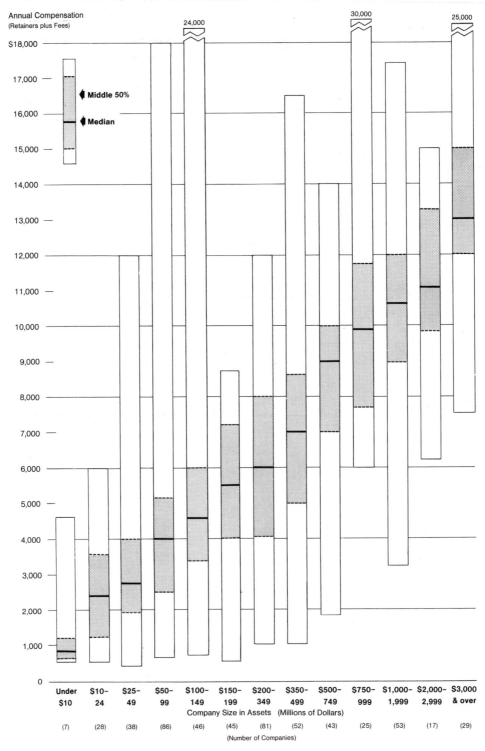

Annual Compensation
(Retainers plus Fees)

Middle 50%

Median

Under $10	$10- 24	$25- 49	$50- 99	$100- 149	$150- 199	$200- 349	$350- 499	$500- 749	$750- 999	$1,000- 1,999	$2,000- 2,999	$3,000 & over
(7)	(28)	(38)	(86)	(46)	(45)	(81)	(52)	(43)	(25)	(53)	(17)	(29)

Company Size in Assets (Millions of Dollars)

(Number of Companies)

4

Chart 3: Annual Compensation of Outside Directors for Regular Board Service, by Industry, 550 Manufacturing Companies

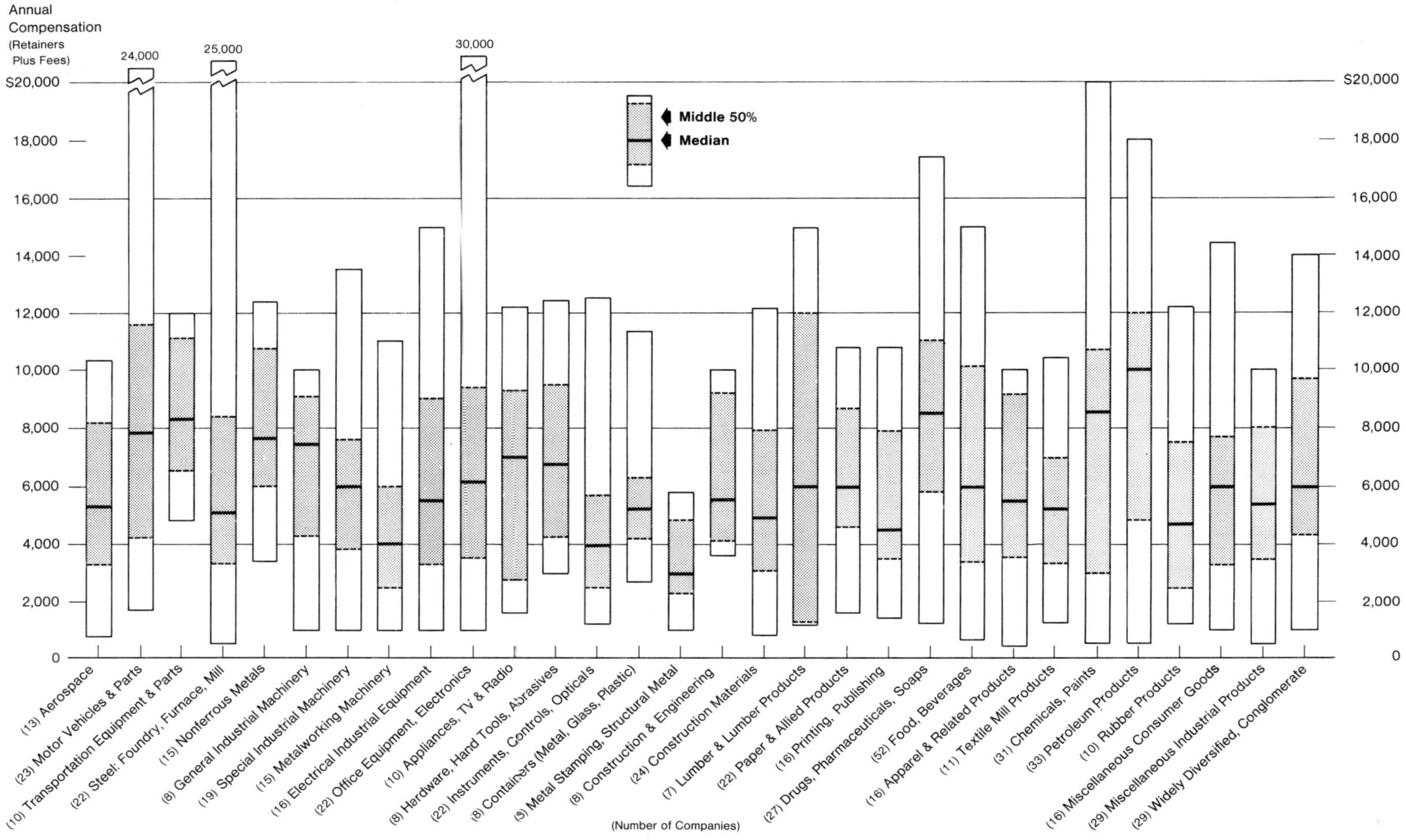
Annual Compensation (Retainers Plus Fees)
$20,000
18,000
16,000
14,000
12,000
10,000
8,000
6,000
4,000
2,000
0
24,000
25,000
30,000
Middle 50%
Median
(13) Aerospace
(23) Motor Vehicles & Parts
(10) Transportation Equipment & Parts
(22) Steel: Foundry, Furnace, Mill
(15) Nonferrous Metals
(8) General Industrial Machinery
(19) Special Industrial Machinery
(15) Metalworking Machinery
(16) Electrical Industrial Equipment
(22) Office Equipment, Electronics
(10) Appliances, TV & Radio
(8) Hardware, Hand Tools, Abrasives
(22) Instruments, Controls, Opticals
(8) Containers (Metal, Glass, Plastic)
(5) Metal Stamping, Structural Metal
(8) Construction & Engineering
(24) Construction Materials
(7) Lumber & Lumber Products
(22) Paper & Allied Products
(16) Printing, Publishing
(27) Drugs, Pharmaceuticals, Soaps
(52) Food, Beverages
(16) Apparel & Related Products
(11) Textile Mill Products
(31) Chemicals, Paints
(33) Petroleum Products
(10) Rubber Products
(16) Miscellaneous Consumer Goods
(29) Miscellaneous Industrial Products
(29) Widely Diversified, Conglomerate
(Number of Companies)

Chart 4: Range of Per-Meeting Fees Paid to Outside Directors

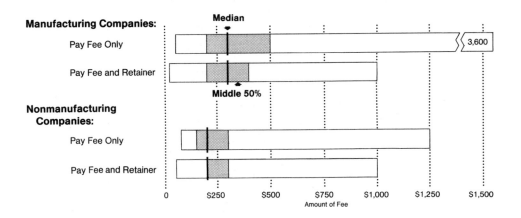

Chart 5: Range of Retainers Paid to Outside Directors

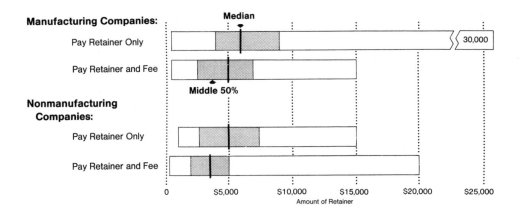

median annual compensation figure for outside directors for regular board service among manufacturing companies with assets of $50 to $99 million was $3,000; the current figure is $4,000, an increase of one-third. For companies in the asset range of $200 to $499 million, the current median annual compensation is $6,100, a 22 percent increase over the 1972 figure of $5,000. Among the largest companies in the two reports—those with assets of a billion dollars and over—the 1975 median figure of $11,500 for annual compensation of outside directors is 28 percent higher than the 1972 median of $9,000.

Measured by industry, increases from one report to the next vary considerably. Comparative figures from eight manufacturing industries appear in Table 2. For information on increases in directors' compensation in nonmanufacturing companies, see page 32.

**Table 2: Increases in Median Annual Compensation for
Outside Directors in Eight Manufacturing Industries**

Industry	Number of Companies (1975)	1975 Median Annual Compensation	Increase Over 1972 Median
Steel	22	$5,050	(Down 6%)
Electrical industrial equipment	16	5,500	15%
Nonferrous metals	15	7,600	17%
Petroleum products	33	10,000	19%
Food, beverages	52	6,000	20%
Printing, printing products, publishing ...	16	4,450	35%
Special industrial machinery	19	6,000	41%
Chemicals, paints	31	8,500	57%

(text continued on page 32)

Table 3: COMPENSATION OF DIRECTORS
570 Manufacturing Companies

Aerospace, Aircraft and Parts

Company	Asset* Group	Regular Board Meetings Per Year	Outside Directors								Employee Directors				Meeting Expense Payment	Honorary Directors Payment
			Regular Meeting Fee	Annual Retainer	Total Potential Annual Compensation for Regular Board Service	Fee, Executive Committee	Retainer, Executive Committee	Fee, Other Committees	Retainer, Other Committees	Compensation for Committee Chairmen If Higher	Regular Meeting Fee	Annual Retainer	Total Potential Annual Compensation for Regular Board Service	Committee Compensation		
1	1	11	200	2400	4600	NC	NC	NC	NC	NC	0	0	0	NC	0	NA
2	1	5	150	0	750	NC	NC	0	0	0	0	0	0	0	ALL	NA
3	2	4	150	2000	2600	NC	NC	0	NC	0	0	0	0	0	VAR[a]	NA
4	2	4	200	0	800	0	0	0	0	0	0	0	0	0	0	O
5	3	7	0	4000	4000	NC	NC	NC	0	0	0	0	0	NE	ALL	NA
6	4	11	300	2000	5300	NC	ND	300	0	0	0	0	0	0	ALL	NA
7	7	8	0	4000	4000	ND	ND	0	0	0	0	0	0	NE	ALL	E
8	6	6	300	4000	5800	NC	NC	300	0	0	0	0	0	0	ALL	500 F
9	8	12	300	5000	8600	300	ND	300	0	0	0	0	0	0	ALL[c]	E
10	11	4	1000	4000	8000	ND	NC	500	0	0	0	0	0	0	ALL	E
11	11	6	500	5000	8000	NC	NC	P[b]	2000[b]	0	0	0	0	0	ALL,	NA
12	11	11	300	5000	8300	300	0	300	0	75000[d]	0	0	0	0	ALL	NA
13	11	11	300	7000	10300	300	0	300	0	0	0	0	0	0	ALL	NA

a – Expenses paid only if travel is required outside headquarters city area
b – Audit and Compensation Committees; $500 fee paid only if committee meets on different day than regular board meeting
c – $300 additional in lieu of travel time if director must travel outside state of residence
c – To chairman of Executive Committee; paid as salary

Motor Vehicles

Company	Asset* Group	Regular Board Meetings Per Year	Regular Meeting Fee	Annual Retainer	Total Potential Annual Compensation for Regular Board Service	Fee, Executive Committee	Retainer, Executive Committee	Fee, Other Committees	Retainer, Other Committees	Compensation for Committee Chairmen If Higher	Regular Meeting Fee	Annual Retainer	Total Potential Annual Compensation for Regular Board Service	Committee Compensation	Meeting Expense Payment	Honorary Directors Payment
1	2	10	50	1200	1700	NC	NC	0	0	NR	0	0	0	0	0	50 F
2	4	13	200	5000	7600	200	0	200	1500	0	0	0	0	0	0	NA
3	4	4	500	4000	6000	ND	ND	250	0	0	0	0	0	0	ALL	NA
4	4	8	0	12000	12000	ND	ND	ND	NC	NC	0	0	0	0	ALL	NA
5	4	5	0	2000	2000	NC	NC	NC	0	0	0	0	0	NC	ALL	S
6	5	4	300	1200	2400	150	0	150	0	0	0	0	0	0	ALL	NA
7	4	4	300	3000	4200[a]	150	0	0	0	0	0	0	0	0	ALL	NA
8	5	12	1000[a]	12000[a]	24000[a]	ND	ND	250	0	0	0	0	0	0	ALL	NA
9	6	6	300	6000	7800	NC	NC	500	0	0	0	0	0	0	ALL	NA
10	6	11	0	6000	6000	ND	0	200	0	0	0	0	0	0	ALL[b]	NA
11	7	8	200	8000	9600	ND	ND	200	0	0	0	0	0	0	ALL	NA
12	7	4	0	3000	3000	NC	NC	0	0	0	0	0	0	0	ALL	NA

(continued)

Co.													
13	7	9	150	4000	5350	150	150	0	150	0	200	1800	O	VAR^c	NA
14	8	6	250	15000^d	16500^d	ND	ND	0	NR	0	0	0	O	ALL	NA
15	9	9	200	0	1800	0	0	1000	0	0	0	0	O	ALL	NA
16	10	6	600	7500	11100	600	600	0	0	0	0	0	O	ALL	NA
17	10	12	400	6000	10800	500	500	0	5000^e	0	0	0	O	O	NR
18	11	12	400	4000	8800	NC	NC	0	0	0	0	0	O	ALL	E
19	11	5	300	6000	7500	300	250	2000	0	0	P	0	P	ALL	NA
20	11	11	400	7200	11600	400^f	300	0	0	0	0	0	O	ALL	NA
21	13	12	250	10000	13000	ND	400	ND	1000^h	15000^g / 10000 / 8000	0	0	O	ALL	NA
22	13	13	300	7500	11400	300	300	0	2500^i	0	0	0	O	ALL	NA
23	13	9	500	7500	12000	500	500	2000	3000^j	0	0	0	O	VAR^k	NA

a — Some directors receive these amounts, but one receives annual consulting fees instead (paid to his firm) of $6,000; another receives per-diem payment
b — Out-of-town directors only
c — $50 flat amount or actual expenses if they are greater
d — Only one director receives retainer; annual compensation for most directors is $1,500
e — Audit, Compensation, Finance Committees
f — No more than two fees (board or committee) paid on any one day
g — $15,000 — Finance Committee; $10,000 — Bonus and Salary Committee; $8,000 — Public Policy Committee; Auditing and Nominating Committees receive $7,000
h — All committees above except Finance Committee
i — Audit Committee; Committee on Compensation and Organization
j — All committees
k — Directors can choose between actual expense reimbursement or flat fee based on distance

Transportation Equipment and Parts

Co.	Grp	Dir												
1	3	12	0	12000	12000	NC	NC	0	0	0	0	0	NE	O	NA
2	3	11	300	1500	4800	0	0	0	0	0	0	0	NE	VAR^a	NA
3	6	4	0	7500	7500	0	0	0	0	0	0	0	0	ALL	NA
4	7	6	200	4800	6000	200	200	0	0	0	0	0	0	ALL	O
5	8	7	0	9000	9000	NC	NC	250	0	0	0	0	0	ALL	O
6	8	4	1000	5000	9000	0	0	1000	0	0	0	0	0	ALL	NA
7	9	4	500	5000	7000	500	500	500	50000^b / 5000	2500	0	0	0	ALL	NA
8	9	6	0	12000	12000	ND	500	ND	0	0	0	0	0	ALL	NA
9	11	11	550	4500	6700	550	550	0	0	0	0	1200	300^c	VAR	NA
10	11	12	200	8400	10800	200	200	0	0	0	0	0	NE	ALL	NA

a — Flat amount, varying with distance traveled, for out-of-town directors only
b — $50,000 — Executive Committee; $5,000 — Audit and Compensation Committees
c — Fee, all committees

NA—Not applicable
NC—No such committee
ND—No outside directors serve
NE—No employee directors serve
NR—No response

A—Flat amount
E—Expenses only
F—Fee
P—Payment made but amount not specified
R—Retainer

S—Same as outside directors
T—Transportation expenses only
VAR—Amounts can vary

*Asset groups ($000,000,000) are:
1—Under 10
2—10 to 24
3—25 to 49
4—50 to 99
5—100 to 149
6—150 to 199
7—200 to 349
8—350 to 499
9—500 to 749
10—750 to 999
11—1 but under 2 billion
12—2 but under 3 billion
13—3 billion and over

Companies within any given asset group are in random order rather than in rank by size.

Table 3: COMPENSATION OF DIRECTORS
570 Manufacturing Companies – Continued

Steel: Foundry, Furnace, Mill

Company	Asset* Group	Outside Directors — Regular Board Meetings Per Year	Regular Meeting Fee	Annual Retainer	Total Potential Annual Compensation for Regular Board Service	Fee, Executive Committee	Retainer, Executive Committee	Fee, Other Committees	Retainer, Other Committees	Compensation for Committee Chairmen If Higher	Employee Directors — Regular Meeting Fee	Annual Retainer	Total Potential Annual Compensation for Regular Board Service	Committee Compensation	Meeting Expense Payment	Honorary Directors Payment
1	2	4	0	3600	3600	0	500	0	500	0	0	0	0	0	ALL	NA
2	3	4	300	0	1200	300	0	300	0	0	0	0	0	0	VAR[a]	NA
3	4	6	0	4000	4000	NC	NC	200	500[b]	0	0	0	0	NE	ALL	NA
4	4	11	200	2000	4200	NC	NC	0	0	0	0	0	0	0	ALL	E
5	4	11	400	0	4400	0	0	0	0	0	0	0	0	NE	ALL	NA
6	4	12	200	0	2400	NC	NC	100	0	0	0	0	0	0	ALL	NA
7	5	13	100	2400	3700	NC	0	100	0	6000[d]	100	0	1300	NE	ALL	NA
8	5	6	0	4000	4000	250[c]	NC	250[c]	0	0	0	0	0	0	ALL	NA
9	6	13	300	3600	7500	150	0	300	0	1600[d]	0	0	0	0	ALL	E
10	6	8	0	500	500	500	0	150[b]	0	0	0	0	0	0	ALL	NA
11	6	NR	0	7500	7500	200	0	500	500	0	0	0	0	0	ALL	NA
12	6	14	200	5200	8000	NC	NC	200[e]	0	0	0	0	0	0	T	NA
13	7	12	0	7500	7500	NC	NC	0	0	0	0	0	0	0	ALL	NA
14	7	5	300	4200	5700	NC	NC	300	0	0	0	0	0	0	O	NA
15	8	5	0	1000	1000	100[f]	0	0	NC	0	0	0	0	0	ALL	NA
16	8	4	100	1000	1400	400[f]	0	400[f]	0	0	0	0	0	0	ALL	NA
17	9	5	400	5000	7000	400	0	400	0	0	0	0	0	0	ALL	NA
18	11	11	400	5000	9400	350	0	350	0	0	0	0	0	0	ALL	NA
19	11	10	350	3000	6500	200	0	200	0	0	0	0	0	0	ALL	NA
20	12	12	200	7500	9900	500	0	500	0	0	0	0	0	0	ALL	200[F]
21	13	11	500	8000	13500	500	0	500	0	0	0	0	0	0	A	NA
22	13	13	500	10000	16500	500	0	500	0	0	0	0	0	0	ALL	NA
23	13	8	0	25000	25000	ND	NC	0	0	0	0	0	0	0	ALL	NA

a – $150, or actual expenses if they are greater
b – Audit Committee
c – Limitation of $1,500 annually in fees for committee service
d – Executive Committee
e – $100 for some committees
f – If meetings are held both morning and afternoon, two fees are paid

Nonferrous Metals

#	Asset group													Outside dir. travel	Employee dir.
1	5	12	0	6000	6000	50a	50a	0	0	0	0	2400	0	ALL	NA
2	6	12	200	5000	7400	200	200	0	0	0	200	0	2400	ALL	NA
3	6	10	0	3600	3600	0	0	0	0	0	300	0	4500	ALL	NA
4	7	7	300	2400	4500	300	300	0	0	2400	300	0	2400	ALL	NA
5	8	4	0	6000	6000	0	0	0	0	0	0	0	0	ALL	NA
6	8	10	0	7500	7500	300	300	0	0	0	0	0	0	ALL	0
7	8	8	325	5000	7600	ND	NC	NC	0	0	0	0	0	ALL	NA
8	10	12	300	5000	8600	200	200	0	300	0	200	3600	200	ALL	NA
9	11	12	0	10000	10000	ND	ND	30000d 20000	0	0	0	0	0	ALL	0
10	11	13	250	7500	10750	250	250	0	0	0	0	0	0	ALL	NA
11	11	12	300	7000	10600	300	300	2000e	0	0	300	3600	300b	ALL	NA
12	12	12	400	7200	12000	300	300	0	0	0	300	3600	0	ALL	0
13	12	12	100	6200	6200	ND	NC	0	0	0	300	1200	0	ALL	NA
14	12	13	400	5000	11200	400	400	0	0	0	100	0	0	VARf	300 F
15	13	12	200	10000	12400	200	200	0	0	0	0	0	0	ALL	3000 R

a — Per hour
b — Executive Committee (per-meeting fee)
c — Fee and retainer for Executive Committee
d — $30,000 for Executive Committee; $20,000 for Audit and Compensation Committees; these amounts *include* $6,000 for regular board service
e — Audit and Pension Investment Committees
f — Travel and accommodation expenses reimbursed for directors who travel more than 20 miles

General Industrial Machinery

#	Asset group													Outside dir. travel	Employee dir.
1	4	5	100	3600	4100	NC	NC	100	0	0	0	0	0	VARa	NA
2	4	5	200	0	1000	0	0	0	0	0	0	0	0	ALL	0
3	5	9	250	2400	4650	250	250	250	0	0	0	0	NE	ALL	S
4	7	6	300	7000	8800	300	300	300	0	0	0	0	0	ALL	NR
5	7	4	0	6000	6000	NC	NC	NC	0	0	0	0	0	ALL	NA
6	7	7	300	7000	9100	300	300	300	1000	0	0	0	0	ALL	NA
7	7	4	0	10000	10000	0	0	0	0	0	0	0	0	ALL	NA
8	11	11	300	7800	9000	300b	300b	300	0	0	0	0	0	ALL	NA

a — Travel and accommodations paid if director must travel a long distance
b — $200 if committee meets on same day as board meeting

NA—Not applicable
NC—No such committee
ND—No outside directors serve
NE—No employee directors serve
NR—No response

A—Flat amount
E—Expenses only
F—Fee
P—Payment made but amount not specified
R—Retainer

S—Same as outside directors
T—Transportation expenses only
VAR—Amounts can vary

* Asset groups ($000,000) are:
1—Under 10
2—10 to 24
3—25 to 49
4—50 to 99
5—100 to 149
6—150 to 199
7—200 to 349
8—350 to 499
9—500 to 749
10—750 to 999
11—1 but under 2 billion
12—2 but under 3 billion
13—3 billion and over

Companies within any given asset group are in random order rather than in rank by size.

Table 3: COMPENSATION OF DIRECTORS
570 Manufacturing Companies – Continued

Special Industrial Machinery

Company	Asset* Group	Reg. Board Meetings Per Year	Regular Meeting Fee	Annual Retainer	Total Potential Annual Comp. for Regular Board Service	Fee, Executive Committee	Retainer, Executive Committee	Fee, Other Committees	Retainer, Other Committees	Comp. for Committee Chairmen If Higher	Emp. Regular Meeting Fee	Emp. Annual Retainer	Emp. Total Potential Annual Comp. for Regular Board Service	Emp. Committee Compensation	Meeting Expense Payment	Honorary Directors Payment
1	1	4	250	0	1000	NC	NC	0	0	0	0	0	0	0	ALL	NA
2	3	6	200	2500	3700	0	0	0	0	0	0	0	0	0	ALL	NA
3	4	6	100	5000	5400	NC	NC	0	0	0	0	0	0	0	ALL	NA
4	4	5	500	5000	7500	300	0	300	0	400[a]	0	0	0	0	ALL	NA
5	5	5	0	13000	13000	0	0	0	0	0	0	0	0	0	ALL	NA
6	5	10	200	3600	5600	ND	ND	100	0	0	0	0	0	0	ALL	NA
7	5	5	0	3000	3000	0	5000	300	0	0	0	0	0	0	ALL	NA
8	5	4	0	6000	6000	NC	NC	0	1000	0	0	0	0	0	ALL	NA
9	5	5	250	1000	2000	NC	ND	250	0	0	250	0	1000	0	ALL	S
10	6	6	400	3600	5600	NC	NC	0	0	0	0	0	0	0	ALL	NA
11	6	9	300	2000[b]	3800	100	NC	100	0	0	100	0	600	0	ALL	NA
12	7	13	300[c]	2000	4700	NC	NC	300[c]	0	0	0	0	0	0	ALL	O
13	7	6	300	3600	7500	NC	NC	300	0	0	0	0	0	0	ALL	NA
14	7	5	300	5000	6800	300	NC	300	0	0	0	0	0	0	ALL	NA
15	7	5	350	5000	6750	0	0	0	0	0	0	0	0	0	ALL	E
16	10	8	200	6000	7600	0[d]	3000	0[d]	0	0	0	0	0	0	ALL	NA
17	10	12	500	6000	12000	500[e]	0	500[e]	1200	0	0	0	0	0	ALL	O
18	11	13	200	6000	8600	NC	NC	200	0	0	200	0	2600	NE	T	NA
19	12	7	500	10000	13500	NC	NC	0	0	0	0	0	0	0	ALL	NA

Metalworking Machinery

Company	Asset* Group	Reg. Board Meetings Per Year	Regular Meeting Fee	Annual Retainer	Total Potential Annual Comp. for Regular Board Service	Fee, Executive Committee	Retainer, Executive Committee	Fee, Other Committees	Retainer, Other Committees	Comp. for Committee Chairmen If Higher	Emp. Regular Meeting Fee	Emp. Annual Retainer	Emp. Total Potential Annual Comp. for Regular Board Service	Emp. Committee Compensation	Meeting Expense Payment	Honorary Directors Payment
1	2	5	200	0	1000	NC	NC	200	NC	NC	0	0	0	NE	0	NA
2	3	12	100	0	1200	NC	NC	NC	NC	NC	100	0	1200	NC	0	NA
3	4	4	400	2000	3600	ND	ND	200	0	0	50	0	200	0	A	NA
4	4	4	0	4000	4000	6000	0	0	0	0	0	0	0	0	ALL	NA
5	4	12	150	2400	4200	7600	0	0	0	0	0	0	0	0	50[a]	NA

a – Audit, Compensation and Pension Committees
b – Paid in $1,000 semi-annual installments, if director has attended three-quarters of the meetings
c – $600 if board or committee meets more than 100 miles from director's place of business
d – A director who attends a committee meeting as an alternate member receives a fee of $200
e – Plus $150 if director attends more than one meeting on the same day

(continued table)

#	*														
6	4	250	1500	2500	250	0	0	0	0	0	0	0		T	O
7	6	200	2500	3700	200[b]	0[b]	0	0	0	0	0	0		ALL	NA
8	6	250	3000	4000	ND	ND	0	0	0	0	0	0		ALL	NA
9	6	500	0	2000	500	500	NC	0	0	0	0	0		T	NA
10	7	100	5000	5400	100	100	0	0	0	0	0	0		T	100 F
11	7	0	7500	7500	250	250	0	0	0	0	0	0		ALL	E
12	8	300	4000	5200	500	10000	0	0	0	0	0	0		ALL	NA
13	8	0	6000	6000	250	0	0	0	0	0	0	0		ALL	NA
14	9	0	10000	10000	250	0	0	0	10000	10000	0	0		ALL	NA
15	12	750	8000	11000	ND	2000	0	15000[c]	0	0	0	0		ALL	NA

a – $25 if director travels only a short distance
b – Would be reduced to $100 if committee were to meet on same day as a board meeting
c – Executive Committee

Electrical Industrial Equipment

#	*														
1	4	0	3000	3000	0	2000	0	0	0	0	0	0		ALL	E
2	2	4200	4200[a]	4200[a]	0	0	0	0	0	0	0	0		0	NA
3	4	250	1200	2200	250	0	0	0	0	0	0	0		ALL	NA
4	5	0	0	0	0	0	0	0	0	0	0	0		NR	NA
5	12	400	3000	4800	NC	NC	NC	0	0	0	0	0		ALL	NA
6	4	0[b]	3000	3000	0[b]	ND	0	0	0	0	0	0		ALL	NA
7	11	250	3600	6350	250	250	0	100	1200	2300	0	0		ALL	4800 R
8	12	250	6000	9000	250	0	0	0	0	0	0	0		T	NA
9	9	C	8000	8000	NC	NC	0	0	0	0	0	0		T	0
10	5	0	5000	5000	0	0	0	0	0	0	0	0		ALL	NA
11	7	300	4200	6000	300	300	NE	0	0	0	0	0		ALL	NA
12	6	200	0	1000	200	2500	0	0	0	0	0	0		ALL	NA
13	8	500	3000	4200	500	1500	1000	0	0	0	0	0		ALL	0
14	9	500	9000	9000	500	1500	1500	0	0	0	0	0		ALL	NA
15	11	500	7500	10000	NC	NC	0	0	0	0	0	0		ALLc	0
16	13	400	8000	11600	400	2000	0	0	0	0	0	0		ALLc	NA
17	13	500	10000	15000	500	500	0	0	0	0	0	0		A	E

a – Actually a monthly amount of $350
b – Per-meeting fee of $500 is paid when meetings of board and committees in a calendar year exceed six
c – For out-of-town meetings only
d – Ranges from $50 to $750, depending on distance

Table 3: COMPENSATION OF DIRECTORS
570 Manufacturing Companies – Continued

Office Equipment, Computers, Electronics

Columns 4–11 (Regular Meeting Fee through Compensation for Committee Chairmen If Higher) fall under **Outside Directors**; columns 12–15 (Regular Meeting Fee through Committee Compensation) fall under **Employee Directors**.

Company	Asset* Group	Regular Board Meetings Per Year	Regular Meeting Fee	Annual Retainer	Total Potential Annual Compensation for Regular Board Service	Fee, Executive Committee	Retainer, Executive Committee	Fee, Other Committees	Retainer, Other Committees	Compensation for Committee Chairmen If Higher	Regular Meeting Fee	Annual Retainer	Total Potential Annual Compensation for Regular Board Service	Committee Compensation	Meeting Expense Payment	Honorary Directors Payment
1	2	5	300	2000	3500	NC	NC	0	0	0	0	0	0		ALL	NA
2	3	12	250	3000	6000	NC	NC	250	0	0	0	0	0	NE	ALL	S
3	3	5	1250	0	6250	500	0	0	0	0	100	0	200	C	ALL	NA
4	3	2	500	0	1000	ND	ND	0	0	0	0	0	0	O	ALL	NA
5	3	4	1000	0	4000	ND	ND	0	0	0	0	0	0	O	ALL	NA
6	3	4	150	1500	2100	NC	NC	225	0	0	P	0	P	NE	ALL	NA
7	4	6	200	4000	5200	0	0	0	0	0	0	0	0	O	VAR^a	NA
8	4	7	500	0	3500	NC	NC	0	0	0	0	0	0	O	ALL	NA
9	5	8	0	4800	4800	0	0	0	0	NR	0	0	0	O	ALL	NA
10	5	8	0	0	0	NC	NC	0	0	0	0	0	0	O	NR	O
11	5	6	400^b	600	3000	ND	ND	0	0	0	0	0	0	O	ALL	NA
12	6	9	0	4500	4500	200	0	0	5000	0	0	0	0	NE	ALL	NA
13	6	10	200	5000	7000	NC	NC	200	0	0	200	0	2000	O	ALL	NA
14	7	12	200	0	2400	0	0	NR	NR	NR	0	0	0	NE	ALL	NA
15	7	6	500	5000	8000	300	0	0	0	0	0	0	0	O	ALL	S
16	7	13	300	6000	9900	NC	NC	0	0	0	0	0	0	NE	ALL	NA
17	7	11	0	8000	8000	300	0	300	2000	0	0	0	0	O	ALL	NA
18	8	11	500	2000	7500	500	0	0	0	0	0	0	0	O	A	NA
19	8	NR	0	10000	10000	200	600	500^c	0	0	0	0	0	O	ALL	NA
20	9	6	400	7500	9900	NC	0	200	2500^f / 1000	Pe	400	0	2400	O	ALL	400 F
21	10	12	0	30000^d	30000	ND	ND	0	0	0	0	0	0	0	ALL	S
22	13	6	0	12000	12000	ND	ND	0	0	0	0	0	0	0	ALL	NA
23	13	11	300	10000	13300	300^g	0	300	0	2000^h / 1000	0	0	0	0	ALL	300 F
24	13	12	350	5000	9200	350	0	350	0	1000	0	0	0	0	ALL^i	NA

a – Transportation including car rental and hotel
b – Average; actual fees are $300 for some directors and $500 for others
c – Audit and Compensation Committees
d – Amount shown is that paid to one class of director for minimum service requirement of 30 days on board business; other payments, depending on kind of director and time spent on board duties, range from $15,000 to $62,500 (payments include time spent on committee assignments)
e – See footnote d; chairmen spend more time and thus receive greater compensation, which is part of the retainer paid for all board services
f – Audit and Stock Option Committees; $1,000 for Executive Compensation Committee
g – $600 if committee meets on different day than board meeting
h – $2,000 for Compensation, Executive and Finance Committees; $1,000 for Audit Committee
i – Precalculated to nearest $25

Appliances, TV and Radio, Housewares

No.	*														
1	4	5	0	3000	3000	ND	ND	0	0	0	0	0	O	ALL	NA
2	4	4	0	1600	1600	0	0	0	0	0	0	0	NE	ALL	O
3	4	5	0	2000	2000	0	10000	ND	0	0	0	0	O	ALL	NA
4	5	5	0	6000	6000	NC	NC	0	0	0	0	0	NE	ALL	NA
5	5	6	500	0	3000	500	500	0	0	0	0	0	O	ALL	E
6	7	7	500	5000	8000	500	500	0	0	0	0	0	O	ALL	NA
7	7	6	500	6000	9000	500	500	0	0	0	0	0	O	ALL	O
8	9	9	0	10000	10000	NC	NC	0	0	2500	0	0	O	ALL	NA
9	9	13	0	9000	9000	NC	NC	0	0	0	0	0	O	ALL	NA
10	13	11	200	10000	12200	0	0	0	0	5000	0	0	O	ALL	NA

a – Expenses paid only for meetings held away from company headquarters

Hardware, Hand Tools, Abrasives

No.	*														
1	5	6	500	3000	6000	250	250	0	0	0	0	0	O	ALL	NA
2	5	5	500	0	3000	0	0	0	0	0	0	0	O	ALL	NA
3	5	11	200	2000	4200	200	1200	0	0	0	0	0	O	ALL	NA
4	7	6	300	8000	9800	300	300	0	0	0	0	0	O	VAR[a]	NA
5	8	8	250	3000	4250	250	0	0	0	0	0	0	O	ALL	NA
6	8	8	300	5000	7400	300	300	0	0	0	0	0	O	ALL	NA
7	8	8	300	10000	12400	300	NC	NC	0	300	2400	0	NE	ALL	NA
8	9	8	300	6000	8400	300	300	0	0	0	0	0	O	ALL	S

Instruments, Controls, Optical Products

No.	*														
1	1	12	100	0	1200	NC	NC	NC	0	0	0	0	NE	ALL	NA
2	2	5	150	500	1250	NC	NC	NC	0	0	0	0	O	ALL	NA
3	3	4	250	5000	6000	250	250	0	0	0	0	0	O	ALL	NA
4	3	8	0	2400	2400	0	0	2400	0	0	0	0	O	ALL	NA
5	3	5	300	0	1500	300	NC	NC	0	0	0	0	O	ALL	NA
6	3	7	300	1200	3300	50	50	0	0	0	0	0	O	ALL	NA
7	4	11	200	2000	4200	200	200	0	200	5000[a]	0	0	O	O	O

NA–Not applicable
NC–No such committee
ND–No outside directors serve
NE–No employee directors serve
NR–No response

A–Flat amount
E–Expenses only
F–Fee
P–Payment made but amount not specified
R–Retainer

S–Same as outside directors
T–Transportation expenses only
VAR–Amounts can vary

* Asset groups ($000,000) are:

1–Under 10	6–150 to 199	11–1 but under 2 billion
2–10 to 24	7–200 to 349	12–2 but under 3 billion
3–25 to 49	8–350 to 499	13–3 billion and over
4–50 to 99	9–500 to 749	
5–100 to 149	10–750 to 999	

Companies within any given asset group are in random order rather than in rank by size.

Table 3: COMPENSATION OF DIRECTORS
570 Manufacturing Companies – Continued

Instruments, Controls, Optical Products - Continued

			Outside Directors								Employee Directors					
Company	Asset* Group	Regular Board Meetings Per Year	Regular Meeting Fee	Annual Retainer	Total Potential Annual Compensation for Regular Board Service	Fee, Executive Committee	Retainer, Executive Committee	Fee, Other Committees	Retainer, Other Committees	Compensation for Committee Chairmen If Higher	Regular Meeting Fee	Annual Retainer	Total Potential Annual Compensation for Regular Board Service	Committee Compensation	Meeting Expense Payment	Honorary Directors Payment
8	4	5	0	2500	2500	NC	NC	0	2500[b] / 1000	0	0	0	0	0	ALL	S
9	4	10	250	2500	5000	NC	NC	250	0	0	250	2500	5000	0	250[c]	NA
10	4	8	0	4800	4800	NC	NC	200	0	0	0	600	600	0	ALL	NA
11	4	10	0	3600	3600	0	0	0	0	25000[a]	0	0	0	0	ALL	NA
12	4	7	400	4000	6800	ND	ND	150	1000	0	0	0	0	0	ALL	NA
13	4	4	100	2000	2400	NC	NC	100	0	0	0	0	0	NE	ALL[d]	NA
14	4	5	150	3000	3750	150	0	150	0	0	100	0	400	0	ALL	NA
15	4	4	100	4000	4400	ND	ND	ND	ND	0	0	0	0	0	ALL	NA
16	5	6	250	2000	3500	250[e]	3000	250[e]	3000[f]	0	0	0	0	0	0	NA
17	5	4	500	3600	5600	NC	NC	0	0	0	0	0	0	0	ALL	0
18	7	11	300	7000	10300	0	0	0	0	0	0	0	0	0	ALL	0
19	7	5	250	3600	4850	200	0	200	0	0	0	0	0	0	ALL	NA
20	8	6	400	1000	3400	200[g]	0	200[g]	0	0	0	0	0	0	ALL	NA
21	8	7	400[h]	5000	7800	400	0	400[i]	0	600[j]	0	0	0	0	ALL	
22	13	5	500	10000	12500	ND	ND	350	0	0	0	0	0	0		

a – Executive Committee
b – $2,500 for Finance Committee; $1,000 for Audit Committee
c – Amounts of $150, $250, and $350 paid, depending on distance traveled
d – 15 cents per mile measured from director's home office
e – $150 if committee meets on same day as board meeting
f – Compensation/Stock Option and Finance/Audit Committees
g – $100 if committee meets on same day as board meeting
h – Local directors receive $200
i – $300 if committee meets on same day as board meeting, or the day previous
j – $400 if committee meets on same day as board meeting, or the day previous

Containers, Packaging (Metal, Glass, Plastic)

Company	Asset* Group	Regular Board Meetings Per Year	Regular Meeting Fee	Annual Retainer	Total Potential Annual Compensation for Regular Board Service	Fee, Executive Committee	Retainer, Executive Committee	Fee, Other Committees	Retainer, Other Committees	Compensation for Committee Chairmen If Higher	Regular Meeting Fee	Annual Retainer	Total Potential Annual Compensation for Regular Board Service	Committee Compensation	Meeting Expense Payment	Honorary Directors Payment
1	3	12	100	1500	2700	100	0	100	0	0	0	0	0	0	VAR[a]	NA
2	3	NR	0	0	0	NC	NC	ND	ND	0	0	0	0	0	ALL	NA
3	3	4	400	3000	4600	400	0	300	0	0	0	0	0	0	ALL	NA
4	4	12	0	0	0	NC	NC	0	0	0	0	0	0	0	200[b]	NA

5	6	4	350	5000	6400	350	0	350	3000	o	o	o	o	o	ALL	S E
6	7	7	200	3200	4000	200	0	200	0	o	o	o	o	o	ALL	
7	7	4	350	4000	5400	350	0	350	0	o	o	o	o	o	ALL	NA
8	8	13	0	5000	5000	0	0	0	0	o	o	o	o	o	ALL	O
9	9	8	250c	4000	6000	250c	600d	250c	0	o	o	o	o	o	ALL	O
10	11	11	300	8000	11300	300	600d	300	0	o	o	o	o	o	ALL	NA

a – Cost of transportation over 50 miles is reimbursed
b – One out-of-town director only
c – Half-day; for full day, any combination of board or committee meetings, $500
d – One committee; for two or more committees, total retainer is $1,200

Metal Stamping, Structural Metal Products

1	1	NR	0	0	0	NC	NC	NC	NC	o	o	o	o	NC	0	NA
2	2	4	0	1000	1000	0	1000	0	1000	o	o	o	o	o	ALL	NA
3	2	12	100	1000	2200	0	0	0	NC	o	o	o	o	o	ALL	NA
4	3	6	0	3000	3000	NC	NC	NC	0	o	o	o	o	o	ALL	NA
5	4	4	0	2500	2500	NC	ND	0	0	o	o	o	o	o	ALL	NA
6	5	6	300	2500	4300	300	0	300	0	o	o	o	o	o	ALL	NA
7	6	9	200	4000	5800	200	0	200	0	o	o	o	o	o	ALL	NA
8	7	10	300	0	3000	300	0	300	0	o	o	o	o	o	ALL	NA
9	8	4	0	5000	5000	NC	ND	0	0	o	o	o	o	o	ALL	O

Construction, Construction Engineering

1	4	4	500	2500	4500	250	0	250	0	o	o	o	o	0	ALL	250 F / 2500 R
2	5	7	300	5000	7100	ND	ND	300a	0	o	o	o	o	0	ALL	NA
3	7	4	1000	0	4000	NC	NC	0	0	o	o	o	o	0	ALL	NA
4	8	10	360	3000	6600	NC	0	100a	0	o	o	o	o	0	85b	NA
5	8	4	200	3600	4400	ND	ND	0	0	o	o	o	o	0	ALL	S
6	5	5	0	3600	3600	ND	ND	0	NC	o	o	o	o	NC	ALL	0
7	8	10	0	10000	10000	ND	ND	NC	0	o	o	o	o	0	ALL	NA
8	10	12	200	7500	9900	200	0	200	0	o	o	o	o	0	ALL	NA

a – Only if committee meets on different day than board meeting
b – $300 paid to one director who travels a great distance

NA—Not applicable
NC—No such committee
ND—No outside directors serve
NE—No employee directors serve
NR—No response

A—Flat amount
E—Expenses only
F—Fee
P—Payment made but amount not specified
R—Retainer

S—Same as outside directors
T—Transportation expenses only
VAR—Amounts can vary

*Asset groups ($000,000) are:
1—Under 10
2—10 to 24
3—25 to 49
4—50 to 99
5—100 to 149
6—150 to 199
7—200 to 349
8—350 to 499
9—500 to 749
10—750 to 999
11—1 but under 2 billion
12—2 but under 3 billion
13—3 billion and over

Companies within any given asset group are in random order rather than in rank by size.

Table 3: COMPENSATION OF DIRECTORS
570 Manufacturing Companies – Continued

Construction Materials and Components (Except Lumber)

Company	Asset* Group	Regular Board Meetings Per Year	Outside Directors — Regular Meeting Fee	Annual Retainer	Total Potential Annual Compensation for Regular Board Service	Fee, Executive Committee	Retainer, Executive Committee	Fee, Other Committees	Retainer, Other Committees	Compensation for Committee Chairmen If Higher	Employee Directors — Regular Meeting Fee	Annual Retainer	Total Potential Annual Compensation for Regular Board Service	Committee Compensation	Meeting Expense Payment	Honorary Directors Payment
1	1	2	150	500	800	0	0	0	0	0	0	500	500	0	ALL	NA
2	2	4	50	2400	2600	0	0	NC	NC	0	50	2400	2600	0	ALL	NA
3	3	4	300	1500	2700	300	0	300	0	0	600	0	3000	300	ALL	NA
4	4	5	600	0	3000	300	0	300	0	0	0	0	0	0	ALL	NA
5	5	12	200	2400	4800	NC	NC	250	0	0	250	0	1250	250	ALLa	O S
6	5	5	250	3000	4250	250	0	200	0	0	0	0	0	0	ALL	NA
7	5	12	200	2400	4800	400	0	300	0	0	0	0	0	0	ALLb	NA
8	5	9	0	3600	3600	NC	NC	300	0	0	0	0	0	0	ALL	NA
9	5	6	500	0	3000	300	0	0	0	0	0	0	0	NE	ALL	NA
10	6	6	400	2400	5200	0	0	150	0	0	0	0	0	0	VARc	NA
11	6	10	150	4200	5700	NC	NC	150	0	0	0	0	0	NE	ALL	NA
12	6	10	250	3000	5500	250	0	200	1000d	0	0	0	0	0	VARe	NA
13	6	6	200	4000	5200	NC	NC	300	0	0	0	0	0	0	ALL	O E
14	7	4	300	2000	3200	300	0	250	0	0	0	0	0	0	ALL	NA
15	7	8	250	3000	5000	250	0	250f	2000g	0	100	0	800	100	ALL	NA
16	7	7	400	5000	7800	ND	ND	ND	500	0	0	0	0	0	ALL	NA
17	7	6	0	8000	8000	300	0	300	1200h	3600i	0	0	0	0	ALL	S 40000 R
18	7	4	0	4000	4000	0	6000	0	800	2400	0	0	0	0	ALL	
19	8	4	500	0	2000	500	NC	500	0	0	0	0	0	0	ALL	NA
20	8	7	700	4000	8900	NC	NC	550	0	0	0	0	0	0	VARj	O
21	9	4	300	8000	9200	300	NC	300	0	0	0	0	0	NE	O T	NA
22	10	10	0	10000	10000	NC	NC	0	0	0	0	0	0	0	ALL	NA
23	11	11	500	6000	11500	200	0	200	0	0	0	0	0	0	ALL	NA
24	11	12	350	8000	12200	350	0	350	0	0	0	0	0	0	ALL	O

a – Paid to directors located out of portion of state in which company is headquartered
b – One European director receives flat amount of $1,000 per meeting
c – If director comes from out of headquarters state; amount depends on location
d – Audit Committee; chairman receives $1,500
e – Flat amount (unspecified) paid if distance is under 100 miles; all actual expenses reimbursed for greater distances
f – Audit Committee; $100 for Stock Option Committee

Lumber and Lumber Products

Co.	AG*	Dir.												Exp.	Emp.
1	4	4	300	0	1200	3C0	0	0	0	12000[a]	0	0	0	ALL	NA
2	4	5	250	0[b]	1250		0	0	0	14400[a]	0	0	0	ALL	NA
3	9	8	0	6000	6000	25	0	0	200	0	200	1600	25	ALL	NA
4	9	6	0	6000	6000	ND	ND	0	0	5000[c]	0	0	0	ALL	NA
5	11	5	400	10000	12000	0	0	0	0	0	0	0	0	ALL	NA
6	12	10	0	8000	8000	500	500	0	0	500[d]	0	0	0	ALL	NA
7	12	10	750	7500	15000	0	500	0	0	3000[e]	0	0	0	VAR[f]	NA

a – Retainer, Executive Committee
b – Board chairman receives $7,200 retainer
c – Executive, Finance and Audit, and Personnel and Organization Committees
d – Fee, Executive Committee
e – Retainer, Audit and Compensation Committees
f – All expenses or $250 if overnight

Paper and Allied Products

Co.	AG*	Dir.													Exp.	Emp.
1	3	4	400	0	1600[a]	200	0	200	0	0	0	0	0	0	ALL	NA
2	4	8	0	6000	6000	NC	NC	0	3000[b]	1500	0	0	NE	0	ALL	NA
3	4	9	300	3000[c]	5700	0	0	200	0	0	100	900	0	0	ALL	NA
4	4	5	200	2000	3000	NC	NC	200	0	0	0	0	NE	0	ALL	NA
5	4	6	300	5000	6800	ND	ND	0	0	0	0	0	0	0	ALL	NA
6	6	4	500	2500	4500	200	0	200	0	0	0	0	0	0	ALL	NA
7	6	7	200	2400	3800	200	0	200	0	0	0	0	0	0	ALL	NA
8	6	4	300	3800	5000	NC	NC	0	0	0	0	0	0	0	ALL	NA
9	7	11	0	4000	4000	0	0	NC	0	0	300	1200	0	0	ALL	NA
10	7	10	0	5000	5000	300	NC	300	0	0	0	0	0	0	0[d]	NA
11	7	8	400	5400	8600	300	300[e]	300	0	0	0	0	0	0	ALL	NA

Table 3: COMPENSATION OF DIRECTORS
570 Manufacturing Companies – Continued

			Outside Directors								Employee Directors					
Company	Asset* Group	Regular Board Meetings Per Year	Regular Meeting Fee	Annual Retainer	Total Potential Annual Compensation for Regular Board Service	Fee, Executive Committee	Retainer, Executive Committee	Fee, Other Committees	Retainer, Other Committees	Compensation for Committee Chairmen If Higher	Regular Meeting Fee	Annual Retainer	Total Potential Annual Compensation for Regular Board Service	Committee Compensation	Meeting Expense Payment	Honorary Directors Payment

Paper and Allied Products - Continued

Company	Asset Group	Mtgs/Yr	Reg Mtg Fee	Annual Retainer	Total Potential	Fee Exec Comm	Retainer Exec Comm	Fee Other Comm	Retainer Other Comm	Comp Comm Chair	Emp Reg Mtg Fee	Emp Annual Retainer	Emp Total	Emp Committee Comp	Meeting Expense	Honorary
12	7	6	1000	0	6000	1000	0	1000	0	0	0	0	0	0	ALL	NA
13	8	5	500	5000	7500	500	0	500	0	0	150	4000	4600	0	ALL	NA
14	8	4	150	4000	4600	150	P	150	NR	0	0	0	0	150	ALL	NA
15	8	5	0	8000	8000	250	0	250	0	0	200	0	1000	0	ALL	NA
16	9	5	200	5000	6000	0	10000	0	1000f	0	0	0	0	0	ALL	NA
17	10	12	200	6000	8400	NC	NC	200	0	0	0	0	0	0	ALL	O
18	10	12	400	4000	8800	400	0	400	0	0	0	0	0	0	ALL	NA
19	11	11	300	7500	10800	NC	NC	250	0	5000g	0	0	0	0	VARh	
20	11	8	300	7200	9600	ND	ND	300i	0	1000	0	0	0	0	ALL	NA
21	11	7	350	8000	10450	ND	ND	350j	0	0	0	0	0	0	ALL	5000 R
22	12	12	400	6000	10800	400	0	400	0	0	0	0	0	0	A	NA

a – Directors receive a minimum of $1,600 even if four meetings are not held
b – $3,000 for Audit Committee; $1,500 for Compensation Committee
c – Paid only if director attends at least one-half of meetings held
d – Expenses are paid only for meetings held at locations other than corporate headquarters
e – $100 if committee meets in conjunction with board meeting
f – Audit Committee
g – $5,000 retainer to one director who chairs both Compensation and Finance Committees; $1,000 to Audit Committee chairman
h – Expense allowances differ according to distance traveled
i – No more than one committee fee paid in the event two or more committees meet on board meeting day
j – Additional fees are not paid if director attends more than one committee meeting on same day

Printing, Printing Products, Publishing

Company	Asset Group	Mtgs/Yr	Reg Mtg Fee	Annual Retainer	Total Potential	Fee Exec Comm	Retainer Exec Comm	Fee Other Comm	Retainer Other Comm	Comp Comm Chair	Emp Reg Mtg Fee	Emp Annual Retainer	Emp Total	Emp Committee Comp	Meeting Expense	Honorary
1	2	12	300	0	3600	NC	NC	150	0	0	0	0	0	NE	T	NA
2	2	12	0	3600	3600	NC	NC	0	0	0	0	0	0	O	O	NA
3	2	4	100	3000	3400	NC	NC	0	0	0	0	0	0	NE	ALL	NA
4	3	5	150	3000	3750	100	0	100	0	0	0	0	0	0	ALL	NA
5	3	4	100	1000	1400	0	0	0	0	0	0	0	0	0	T	NA
6	3	4	0	3000	3000	NC	NC	100	0	0	0	0	0	0	ALL	NA
7	5	6	350	2400	4500	NC	NC	350	0	0	0	0	0	0	ALL	NA

8	5	4	500	4000	6000	200	0	200	0	0	0	0	0	0	ALL	NA
9	5	4	250	2000	3000	125	0	125	0	0	0	0	0	0	VAR[a]	NA
10	7	6	200	6000	7200	NC	NC	200	0	0	0	0	0	0	ALL	NA
11	7	7	0	10000	10000	200	0	200	0	0	0	0	0	0	ALL	250 F
12	7	11	400	0	4400	NC	NC	400	0	0	0	0	0	0	ALL	S
13	8	11	0	7500	7500	0	0	250	0	0	0	0	0	0	ALL	NA
14	8	8	600	6000	10800	600[b]	0	600[c]	0	0	0	0	0	0	ALL	NA
15	9	4	500	6000	8000	500	0	500	0	0	0	0	0	0	ALL	S
16	9	12	0	10000	10000	400[d]	0	400[d]	0	0	0	0	0	0	ALL	NA

a – All expenses paid if board meets away from headquarters
b – Only if committee meets on different day than board meeting
c – $200 on same day as another meeting
d – $200 if same day as board meeting

Drugs, Pharmaceuticals, Cosmetics, Soaps

1	2	4	400	0	1600	0	0	0	0	0	0	0	0	0	ALL	NA
2	3	10	200	0	2000	NC	NC	200	0	0	100	0	1000	200	ALL	S
3	4	4	300	0	1200	NC	NC	0	0	0	300	0	1200	NE	ALL	NA
4	5	8	500	6000	10000	NC	NC	500	0	0	0	0	0	0	ALL	NA
5	6	11	0	6000	6000	NC	NC	0	1000	500[a]	0	6000	6000	NE	0	NA
6	6	9	400	4800	8400	NC	NC	400	0	0	0	0	0	0	ALL	NA
7	6	4	250	3000	4000	NC	NC	0	0	0	0	0	0	0	T	NA
8	8	11	250	2000	4750	250	0	250	0	0	0	0	0	0	0	0
9	8	10	200	5000	7000	NC	NC	NC	NC	NC	0	0	0	NC	ALL	NR
10	8	10	500	6000	11000	NC	NC	300	15000[b]	500[c]	0	0	0	0	ALL	NA
										25000						
										10000						
11	8	8	100	5000	5800	ND	ND	100	0	150[d]	0	0	0	0	ALL	NA
12	8	11	300	6000	9300	300	0	300	0	0	0	0	0	0	ALL	NA
13	9	10	200	10000	12000	0	1000	0	1000	0	200	0	2000	0	ALL	7500 R
14	9	8	300	6000	8400	0	0	300	0	0	0	0	0	0	ALL	NA
15	9	10	0	6500	6500	ND	ND	0	0	0	0	0	0	0	0	NA
16	9	9	500	1200	5700	0	0	0	0	0	0	0	0	0	ALL	NA
17	9	11	300	7500	10800	NC	NC	0	2500[e]	3000[f]	0	0	0	0	ALL	NA
									1000	1500						
18	9	6	600	5000[g]	8600	NC	NC	0	0	0	0	0	0	0	ALL	NA

NA–Not applicable
NC–No such committee
ND–No outside directors serve
NE–No employee directors serve
NR–No response

A–Flat amount
E–Expenses only
F–Fee
P–Payment made but amount not specified
R–Retainer

S–Same as outside directors
T–Transportation expenses only
VAR–Amounts can vary

*Asset groups ($000,000) are:
1–Under 10
2–10 to 24
3–25 to 49
4–50 to 99
5–100 to 149
6–150 to 199
7–200 to 349
8–350 to 499
9–500 to 749
10–750 to 999
11–1 but under 2 billion
12–2 but under 3 billion
13–3 billion and over

Companies within any given asset group are in random order rather than in rank by size.

Table 3: COMPENSATION OF DIRECTORS
570 Manufacturing Companies – Continued

Drugs, Pharmaceuticals, Cosmetics, Soaps – Continued

			Outside Directors								Employee Directors					
Company	Asset* Group	Regular Board Meetings Per Year	Regular Meeting Fee	Annual Retainer	Total Potential Annual Compensation for Regular Board Service	Fee, Executive Committee	Retainer, Executive Committee	Fee, Other Committees	Retainer, Other Committees	Compensation for Committee Chairmen If Higher	Regular Meeting Fee	Annual Retainer	Total Potential Annual Compensation for Regular Board Service	Committee Compensation	Meeting Expense Payment	Honorary Directors Payment
19	9	12	100	7500	8700	0	0	200	0	0	100	0	1200	0	ALL	7500 R
20	9	5	400h	6000	8000	0	0	400h	0	2000i	0	0	0	0	ALL	NA
21	10	7	400	10000	12800	500	0	500	0	P	0	0	0	0	ALL	NA
22	11	9	300	7500	10200	300	2500	300	0	0	0	0	0	0	ALL	S
23	11	10	400	10000	14000	400	0	400	0	0	0	0	0	0	T	NA
24	11	12	250	14400	17400	ND	ND	0	1200	0	0	0	0	0	0	NA
25	11	10	350	8000	11500	350	2000	350	0	1000j	0	0	0	NE	ALL	NA
26	11	11	600	7000	13600	ND	ND	250	0	350k	0	0	0	0	ALL	NA
27	11	11	300	5000	8300	200l	0	200l	0	75000 m / 50000 / 25000	0	0	0	0	ALL	NA
28	11	4	ND	ND	ND	ND	ND	ND	ND	0	0	0	0	0	NA	NA

a — Retainer, Audit Committee, Officers' Compensation and Stock Option Committee
b — Members of Finance Committee receive $15,000 retainers; members of other committees receive $300 meeting fee
c — $500 per-meeting fee for Compensation and Stock Option Committees; retainers of $25,000 for Finance Committee, $10,000 for Audit Committee
d — Per-meeting fee to committee chairmen who are outside directors
e — $2,500 for Compensation and Finance Committee; $1,000 for Audit Committee
f — $3,000 retainer for Finance Committee; $1,500 for Audit Committee
g — Two directors who also have consulting arrangements receive approximately $25,000
h — $200 if meeting is in greater metropolitan area in which director resides
i — Retainer, Audit and Compensation Committees
j — Retainer, Audit and Finance Committees
k — Per-meeting fee, Audit Committee
l — $100 if committee meets on same day as board meeting
m — $75,000 for Executive Committee; $50,000 for Compensation Committee; $25,000 for Audit and Directors Committees

Food, Beverages and Kindred Products

			Outside Directors								Employee Directors					
Company	Asset* Group	Regular Board Meetings Per Year	Regular Meeting Fee	Annual Retainer	Total Potential Annual Compensation for Regular Board Service	Fee, Executive Committee	Retainer, Executive Committee	Fee, Other Committees	Retainer, Other Committees	Compensation for Committee Chairmen If Higher	Regular Meeting Fee	Annual Retainer	Total Potential Annual Compensation for Regular Board Service	Committee Compensation	Meeting Expense Payment	Honorary Directors Payment
1	2	8	100	0	800	NC	NC	NC	NC	NC	100	0	800	NC	0	NA
2	2	4	500	2000	4000	NC	NC	NC	NC	NC	NR	NR	P	NC	0	O
3	2	12	100	0	1200	0	0	0	0	0	0	0	0	NE	0	NA
4	4	11	0	6000	6000	NC	NC	100	0	0	0	0	0	NE	0	NA
5	4	6	200	1500	2700	200	0	200	0	0	0	0	0	0	ALL	

No.	AG	Dir	M1	M2	M3	C4	C5	C6	C7	C8	C9	C10	C11	C12	C13	C14
6	4	6	100	0	600	NC	NC	0	0	0	0	0	0	NE	ALL	NA
7	4	4	300	3600	4800	NC	NC	300	0	0	0	0	0	NE	ALL	NA
8	4	12	300	3600	7200	300	300	ND	ND	0	0	0	0	0	ALL	NA
9	4	5	150	2500	3250	0	0	NC	NC	0	0	0	0	0	0	NA
10	4	5	250	0	1250	NC	NC	NC	ND	0	0	0	0	NC	0	O
11	4	6	200	1200	2400	ND	ND	NC	NC	0	0	0	0	0	ALL	NA
12	4	13	200	8000	8000	0	7000	300	20000a	0	0	0	0	0	ALL	O
13	5	4	0	0	650	0	0	50	0	NE	NE	NE	NE	NE	ALL	NR
14	5	7	50	1800	3800	500	0	300	0	0	0	0	0	0	ALL	O
15	5	NR	500	0	4900	0	ND	250	0	0	0	0	0	0	NA	NA
16	5	9	700	10000	10000	0	ND	0	0	1200	1200	1200	0	0	ALL	O
17	5	7	ND	ND	ND	ND	ND	ND	0	0	0	0	0	0	ALL	S
18	6	10	0	0	1750	ND	ND	0	0	0	0	0	0	0	ALL	NA
19	6	4	250	2500	4500	0	0	200	0	200	1200	1200	0	0	ALL	O
20	6	11	200	4000	5600	200	200	200	1800b	0	0	0	0	0	ALL	S
21	6	11	400	6000	6000	400	1800	400	18900c / 1800	0	0	0	0	0	ALL	O
22	6	6	0	6000	6000	ND	ND	0	0	0	0	0	0	0	ALL	200 F
23	6	6	500	2500	5500	250	250	250	0	0	0	0	0	0	0	NA
24	6	4	250	1200	2200	NC	NC	NC	NC	0	0	0	0	NC	ALL	NA
25	7	12	200	4000	5200	200	200	200	NC	200	1200	1200	0	0	ALL	NA
26	7	5	200	2400	2400	ND	ND	ND	6000	0	0	0	0	0	ALL	NA
27	7	10	250	4800	5800	NC	NC	200d	0	0	0	0	0	0	ALL	S
28	7	6	400	0	2500	ND	ND	150	0	0	0	0	0	0	ALL	NA
29	7	6	0	4000	6400	ND	ND	400	0	0	0	0	0	0	ALL	S
30	7	5	200	12000	12000	0	0	0	0	0	0	0	0	0	ALL	S
31	7	12	0	6000	7000	NC	NC	ND	0	0	0	0	0	0	ALL	NA
32	8	8	200	8000	8000	NC	NC	NC	0	0	0	0	NE	NE	ALL	NA
33	8	5	1000	9000	11400	2000	2000	200	0	0	0	0	NE	NE	VARe	O
34	8	12	200	0	5000	200	200	200	0	0	0	0	0	0	ALL	E
35	8	5	500	2500	5000	ND	ND	500	0	0	0	0	0	0	ALL	S
36	8	12	500	2500	8500	ND	ND	250	0	0	0	0	0	0	ALL	NA
37	9	6	300	5000	6800	300	0	300	0	0	0	0	0	0	ALL	S
38	9	12	300	3500	7100	NC	NC	300	0	0	0	0	0	0	ALL	NA
39	9	4	250	3000	4000	NC	NC	0	0	0	0	0	0	0	ALL	NA
40	9	NR	0	15000	15000	0	10000	10000	0	0	0	0	0	0	ALL	O
41	10	6	500	7500	10500	ND	ND	250	0	0	0	0	0	0	ALL	O
42	10	12	500	6000	12000	NC	NC	500	0	0	0	0	0	0	ALL	NA
43	10	11	300	3600	6900	NC	2400	100	0	0	0	0	0	0	175f	N/.
44	10	12	400	10000	14800	ND	ND	400	0	0	0	0	0	0	ALL	NA

NA—Not applicable
NC—No such committee
ND—No outside directors serve
NE—No employee directors serve
NR—No response

A—Flat amount
E—Expenses only
F—Fee
P—Payment made but amount not specified
R—Retainer

S—Same as outside directors
T—Transportation expenses only
VAR—Amounts can vary

* Asset groups ($000,000) are:
1—Under 10
2—10 to 24
3—25 to 49
4—50 to 99
5—100 to 149
6—150 to 199
7—200 to 349
8—350 to 499
9—500 to 749
10—750 to 999
11—1 but under 2 billion
12—2 but under 3 billion
13—3 billion and over

Companies within any given asset group are in random order rather than in rank by size.

Table 3: COMPENSATION OF DIRECTORS
570 Manufacturing Companies – Continued

Food, Beverages and Kindred Products - Continued

Company	Asset* Group	Regular Board Meetings Per Year	Outside Directors — Regular Meeting Fee	Annual Retainer	Total Potential Annual Compensation for Regular Board Service	Fee, Executive Committee	Retainer, Executive Committee	Fee, Other Committees	Retainer, Other Committees	Compensation for Committee Chairmen If Higher	Employee Directors — Regular Meeting Fee	Annual Retainer	Total Potential Annual Compensation for Regular Board Service	Committee Compensation	Meeting Expense Payment	Honorary Directors Payment
45	11	11	250	5000	7750	250	1500	200	0	0	0	0	0	0	ALL	NA
46	11	11	200	10000	12200	200	0	200	0	0	0	0	0	0	ALL	10000 R
47	11	12	300	10000	13600	300	0	300	0	0	0	0	0	0	ALL	NA
48	11	11	500	8000	13500	500	0	500	0	0	0	0	0	0	ALL	0
49	11	11	200	10000	12200			200	0	0	0	0	0	0	ALL	
50	11	12	200	6500	8900	100	3000	100	0	200g	200	0	2400	0	ALL	200 F
51	11	12	500	7500	13500	500h	0	500h	0	0	0	0	0	0	ALL	NA
52	11	9	400	10000	13600	400	0	400	0	600i	0	0	0	0	ALL	NA
53	11	4	800	0	3200	400	0	400	0	0	0	0	0	0	ALL	NA
54	12	12	250	12000	15000	250	0	250j	0	500k	0	0	0	0	ALL	S
55	13	13	250	10000	13250	ND	ND	250l	0		0	0	0	0	ALL	NA

a – Executive Committee
b – Audit, Compensation-Stock Option Committees
c – $18,900 for Executive Committee; $1,800 for Audit Committee
d – $100 if committee meets on same day as board meeting
e – One director receives a flat amount (unspecified), others receive actual expenses
f – $300 if distance traveled is greater than 200 miles
g – Audit and Officer Compensation Committees
h – $200 if committee meets on same day as board meeting
i – Per-meeting fee for Audit, Compensation, Executive Committees
j – For some committees the fee is $200
k – $400 for committees where regular fee is $200
l – $500 if committee meets on different day than board meeting

Apparel and Related Products

Company	Asset* Group	Regular Board Meetings Per Year	Outside Directors — Regular Meeting Fee	Annual Retainer	Total Potential Annual Compensation for Regular Board Service	Fee, Executive Committee	Retainer, Executive Committee	Fee, Other Committees	Retainer, Other Committees	Compensation for Committee Chairmen If Higher	Employee Directors — Regular Meeting Fee	Annual Retainer	Total Potential Annual Compensation for Regular Board Service	Committee Compensation	Meeting Expense Payment	Honorary Directors Payment
1	3	4	100	0	400	ND	ND	NC	NC	0	0	0	0	0	ALL	NA
2	3	4	500	0	2000	NC	NC	0	0	0	0	0	0	0	ALL	NA
3	4	4	200	3000	3800	100	0	100	0	0	0	0	0	NE	0	NA
4	4	12	100	2500	3700	NC	NC	0	0	0	0	0	0	0	ALL	S
5	5	6	500	7000	10000	ND	ND	500	0	0	0	0	0	0	ALL	0
6	6	6	0	5000	5000	500	0	500	0	0	50	0	300	0	VAR a	NA
7	7	6	300	7500	9300	500	0	300	0	0	0	0	0	0	0	NA
8	7	4	250	0	1000	ND	ND	NC	NC	0	0	0	0	0		

Co.	Asset																
9	7	10	250	0	7500	10000	250	0	0	0	0	0	0	ALL	0	NA
10	7	6	500	NC	2000	5000	500	NC	0	0	0	0	0	ALL	0	NA
11	7	10	200		5500	7500	100^b	NC	0	0	0	0	0	ALL	NE	50 F
12	7	4	500	ND	4000	6000	250^c	ND	0	0	0	0	0	ALL	0	1000 E
13	7	5	250	ND	7500	8750	250	ND	0	0	0	0	0	ALL	0	O
14	7	4	100	ND	NR^d	NR	NR	ND	0	0	0	0	0	ALL	0	NA
15	8	5	200	NC	2500	3500	200	ND	0	0	0	0	0	ALL	0	100 F
16	9	10	0	NC	7500	7500	0	NC	0	0	0	0	0	ALL	0	NA
17	9	12	400	O	4800	9600	200	O	0	0	0	0	0	ALL	0	NA

a – Allowance varies according to distance traveled
b – $200 if committee meets on different day than board meeting
c – $500 if committee meets on different day than board meeting
d – Retainers vary considerably among directors

Textile Mill Products

Co.	Asset																
1	2	5	250	0	ND	1250	250	ND	250	0	0	0	0	ALL	0	NA
2	3	4	0	10000	O	10000	O	NC	0	0	0	0	0	ALL	O	NA
3	4	5	400	2400	NC	4400	NC	300	2000	400	0	0	NE	ALL	NE	NA
4	5	7	400	4000	NC	6800	NC	200^a	0	0	0	600	NE	ALL	NE	O
5	4	4	400	0	ND	1600	O	100	400	100	0	0	0	ALL	0	NA
6	5	8	200	2400	NC	4000	O	0	0	0	0	0	O	O	O	O
7	5	6	200	4000	O	5200	NC	200	120	20	0	NC	20	ALL	20	NA
8	7	4	200	2500	NC	3300	200	0	0	0	0	0	0	O	O	NA
9	8	NR	0	7200	200	7200	200	200	0	0	400^b	0	0	ALL	0	NR
10	8	7	300	4000	300	6100	300	300^c	0	0	7500^d	0	0	ALL	0	
11	10	10	200	5000	ND	7000	ND	200	0	0	1500	0	0	ALL	0	200 F
12	11	9	600^e	5000	600	10400	600^f	600	0	0	25000^g	0	0	ALL	0	NA

a – $400 if committee meets on different day than board meeting
b – Fee paid to chairmen of all committees except Executive Committee
c – Paid only for committee meetings that are other than routine
d – $7,500 for Executive Committee; $1,500 for Audit and Compensation Committees
e – $300 for meetings no further than 100 miles from director's residence
f – $300 if meeting is held on same day as another meeting
g – Finance Committee

NA–Not applicable
NC–No such committee
ND–No outside directors serve
NE–No employee directors serve
NR–No response

A–Flat amount
E–Expenses only
F–Fee
P–Payment made but amount not specified
R–Retainer

S–Same as outside directors
T–Transportation expenses only
VAR–Amounts can vary

*Asset groups ($000,000) are:
1–Under 10
2–10 to 24
3–25 to 49
4–50 to 99
5–100 to 149
6–150 to 199
7–200 to 349
8–350 to 499
9–500 to 749
10–750 to 999
11–1 but under 2 billion
12–2 but under 3 billion
13–3 billion and over

Companies within any given asset group are in random order rather than in rank by size.

Table 3: COMPENSATION OF DIRECTORS
570 Manufacturing Companies – Continued

Chemicals, Paints and Allied Products

Company	Asset* Group	Regular Board Meetings Per Year	Outside Directors								Employee Directors				Meeting Expense Payment	Honorary Directors Payment
			Regular Meeting Fee	Annual Retainer	Total Potential Annual Compensation for Regular Board Service	Fee, Executive Committee	Retainer, Executive Committee	Fee, Other Committees	Retainer, Other Committees	Compensation for Committee Chairmen If Higher	Regular Meeting Fee	Annual Retainer	Total Potential Annual Compensation for Regular Board Service	Committee Compensation		
1	2	6	0	1200	1200	NC	NC	0	0	0	0	0	0	NE	ALL	NA
2	2	8	250	1000	3000	0	0	250	0	0	0	0	0	0	O	NA
3	2	5	100	0	500	100	0	0	0	0	0	0	0	0	ALL	NA
4	3	6	200	2000	3200	75	400	100	0	0	0	0	0	NE	ALL	S
5	3	8	200	1000	2600	NC	NC	100	0	0	0	0	0	0	ALL	NA
6	4	5	3600	0	18000	0	0	0	0	0	0	0	0	0	ALL	NA
7	4	4	500	0	2000	500	0	NR	0	0	500	0	2000	0	ALL	NR
8	5	4	400	0	1600	ND	ND	400	0	0	0	0	0	0	ALL	NA
9	6	4	0	7500	7500	0	5000	0	0	18500[a]	0	0	0	0	ALL	NA
10	6	4	400	2400	4000	200	0	200	0	0	0	0	0	0	ALL	NA
11	7	5	300	1500	3000	100	0	100	0	0	0	0	0	0	ALL	NA
12	7	11	250	5000	7750	250	0	250	0	0	0	0	0	0	ALL	NA
13	7	7	200	1000	2400	0	0	200	0	0	0	0	0	0	T	200 F
14	7	7	250	5000	6750	500	2500	0	1000	0	0	0	0	0	ALL	NA
15	9	5	500	6000	8500	500	2000	250	0	0	0	0	0	0	ALL	NA
16	9	5	500	8000	10500	ND	0	500	0	0	0	0	0	0	ALL	E
17	9	12	0	10000	10000	ND	ND	300	0	2000	0	0	0	0	ALL	NA
18	9	6	300	8000	9800	300	ND	300	0	0	0	0	0	0	ALL	O
19	9	9	300	8000	10700	ND	ND	300[b]	0	0	0	0	0	0	ALL	NA
20	10	13	300	6000	9900	200	ND	500	0	0	0	0	0	0	ALL	NA
21	10	9	400	6000	9600	0	0	200	0	0	0	0	0	0	ALL	NA
22	10	12	0	7000	7000	ND	ND	200[c]	0	0	0	0	0	0	ALL	NA
23	11	12	500	0	6000	ND	ND	500	0	0	0	0	0	0	ALL	NA
24	11	12	300	8000	11600	ND	ND	300	0	10000[d]	100	0	1200	0	ALL	NA
25	11	13	650	5000	13450	ND	0	650[e]	0	0	0	0	0	0	ALL	NR
26	11	10	400	7000	11000	300	0	200	0	0	0	0	0	0	ALL	NA
27	11	9	300	8000	10700	NC	NC	300	0	2000	0	0	0	0	ALL	S
28	12	12	800	0	9600	ND	ND	200	0	0	0	0	0	0	ALL	NA
29	13	11	0	20000[f]	20000	ND	ND	0	21000[g]	18000[h]	0	0	0	0	ALL	NA
30	13	12	100	12000	13200	ND	ND	0	15000	21000 / 90000	0	0	0	0	VAR	NA
31	13	10	400	12000	16000	400	0	400	0	0	0	0	0	0	VAR[i]	NA

Petroleum Products

#	Asset group												
1	1	4	0	0	0	0	0	0	0	0	600	0	T / NA
2	1	6	100	0	600	0	0	200	0	100	800	0	O / NA
3	2	4	200	2500a	3300	200	0	200	0	200	0	200	ALL / NA
4	2	5	100	0	500	NC	NC	NC	0	0	0	0	ALL / NA
5	3	4	250	0	1000	NC	NC	0	0	0	0	NE	ALL / NA
6	4	6	250	4800	1000	NC	12500	0	0	0	0	0	NR / O
7	4	4	0	0	4800	0	0	0	0	0	0	0	ALL / NA
8	4	5	0	5000	0	0	0	0	0	0	0	0	ALL / NA
9	5	6	0	8000	5000	ND	ND	0	0	0	0	0	ALL / NA
10	6	12	500	0	11000	NC	NC	0	0	0	1200	0	ALL / NA
11	6	12	100	2400	1200	0	0	100	0	100	0	0	ALL / NA
12	6	12	200	10000	4800	200	ND	100	0	100	P	0	ALL / NA
13	7	4	0	1500	10000	NC	ND	NC	12000b	0	NR	0	ALL / NA
14	7	4	300	5000	2700	ND	ND	0	0	0	0	0	ALL / NA
15	8	6	500	5000	7000	250	0	250	0	0	0	0	ALL / NA
16	8	4	300	8000	6200	200	0	200	0	0	0	0	ALL / NA
17	9	6	400	7500	10400	400	0	400	0	400	2400	400	ALL / NA
18	9	12	300	15000	11100	200	0	200	0	0	0	0	ALL / S
19	10	6	0	15000	15000	ND	0	0	0	0	0	0	ALL / NA
20	11	7	0	5000c	5000	0	ND	0	0	0	0d	0	ALL / NA
21	11	10	0	10000	10000	ND	ND	0	0	0	0	0	ALL / S
22	11	4	0	9000	9000	300	ND	0	0	0	0	0	ALL / NA
23	12	12	500	6000	12000	500e	0	500e	0	0	1300	0	ALL / NA
24	12	13	100	10000	11300	100	0	100	0	100	0	100	ALL / NA
25	12	12	300	7500	11100	300	ND	300	0	0	0	0	ALL / NA
26	13	6	500	15000	18000	500	0	500	0	0	0	0	ALL / 3000 R

Table 3: COMPENSATION OF DIRECTORS
570 Manufacturing Companies – Continued

Company	Asset* Group	Regular Board Meetings Per Year	Outside Directors								Employee Directors				Meeting Expense Payment	Honorary Directors Payment
			Regular Meeting Fee	Annual Retainer	Total Potential Annual Compensation for Regular Board Service	Fee, Executive Committee	Retainer, Executive Committee	Fee, Other Committees	Retainer, Other Committees	Compensation for Committee Chairmen If Higher	Regular Meeting Fee	Annual Retainer	Total Potential Annual Compensation for Regular Board Service	Committee Compensation		

Petroleum Products – Continued

Company	Asset* Group	Reg. Bd. Mtgs/Yr	OD Reg. Mtg. Fee	OD Annual Retainer	OD Total Potential	OD Fee, Exec. Comm.	OD Retainer, Exec. Comm.	OD Fee, Other Comm.	OD Retainer, Other Comm.	OD Comp. Chairmen If Higher	ED Reg. Mtg. Fee	ED Annual Retainer	ED Total Potential	ED Committee Comp.	Meeting Expense Payment	Honorary Directors Payment
27	13	13	300	10000	13900	250	0	250	0	0	0	0	0	0	ALL	NA
28	13	7	0	7500	7500	NC	NC	250[f]	0	0	0	0	0	NE	ALL	NA
29	13	12	500	6000	12000	ND	ND	250[f]	0	0	0	0	0	0	ALL	NA
30	13	12	400	10000	14000	400	0	400	0	0	0	0	0	0	ALL	NA
31	13	5	400	10000	12000	400	0	400	0	0	0	0	0	0	ALL	3000 R
32	13	10	500	10000	15000	400	0	300[g]	0	500[h]	500	0	5000	400	ALL	NA
33	13	13	0	15000	15000	ND	ND	0	0	2500	0	0	0	0	ALL	NA
34	13	11	500	6000	11500	500	0	500	0	0	0	6000	11500	500	ALL	NA
35	13	12	0	12000	12000	ND	ND	300	1200	0	0	0	0	0	ALL	NA

a – Paid only if director attends at least two-thirds of meetings
b – Executive Committee
c – Maximum; other retainers range as low as $2,500
d – Not compensated as directors but compensation range as employees is $7,500 higher than for nondirector employees
e – $300 if committee meets on same day as board meeting
f – $100 if committee meets on same day as board meeting
g – $1,000 for Committee of Nonmanagement Directors
h – $2,500 for Committee of Nonmanagement Directors; $500 for Auditing Committee (per-meeting fees)

Rubber Products

Company	Asset* Group	Reg. Bd. Mtgs/Yr	OD Reg. Mtg. Fee	OD Annual Retainer	OD Total Potential	OD Fee, Exec. Comm.	OD Retainer, Exec. Comm.	OD Fee, Other Comm.	OD Retainer, Other Comm.	OD Comp. Chairmen If Higher	ED Reg. Mtg. Fee	ED Annual Retainer	ED Total Potential	ED Committee Comp.	Meeting Expense Payment	Honorary Directors Payment
1	2	6	200	0	1200	0	0	0	0	0	100	0	600	0	0	NA
2	2	4	0	6000	6000	0	0	0	0	0	0	0	0	0	ALL	NA
3	3	13	100	1000	2300	100	0	0	0	0	0	0	0	0	ALL	NA
4	4	6	250	1000	2500	NC	NC	250	NC	0	0	0	0	0	ALL	NA
5	4	5	0	4800	4800	0	18167	NC	0	24000[a]	0	4800	4800	0	ALL	NA
6	4	5	300	3600	5100	300	0	300	0	0	0	0	0	0	ALL	NA
7	6	5	300	3000	4500	300	0	250	0	0	0	0	0	0	ALL	NA
8	7	4	250	3500	4500	250	0	200	0	0	0	0	0	0	0	NA
9	11	11	200	10000	12200	0	0	250	0	0	0	0	0	0	ALL	NA
10	11	6	0	12000	12000	ND	ND	250	0	0	0	0	0	0	ALL	500 F

a – Executive Committee

Miscellaneous Consumer Products

No.																
1	3	10	0	4000	4000	100	0	50	0	0	100	0	1000	20[a] 50	ALL	NA
2	3	4	500	0	2000	ND	0	0	ND	0	0	0	0	0	ALL	NA
3	4	6	400	0	2400	NC	100	0	0	0	0	2400	0	0	0	NA
4	4	6	NR	7500	NR	NR	NC	NC	0	0	2400	0	0	NE	T	NA
5	4	4	3000	3000	3000	200	200	200	NC	0	0	0	0	0	ALL	O
6	4	5	250	4000	5250	250	0	250	0	6000[b] 1000	0	0	0	0	ALL	NA
7	4	6	0	5000	5000	NC	0	0	5000	0	0	0	0	0	ALL	NA
8	4	4	250	0	1000	ND	0	ND	0	0	0	0	0	0	0	E
9	5	6	ND	ND	ND	ND	ND	0	ND	0	0	0	0	0	NA	O
10	7	10	500	3000	6000	NC	300	ND	NR	500	0	0	0	0	ALL	NA
11	7	5	200	6000	8000	200	200	300	0	0	0	0	0	0	T	NA
12	7	5	500	6000	6000	500	500	200	0	0	0	0	0	0	ALL	NA
13	8	10	500	5000	7500	300	0	500	0	0	0	0	0	0	VAR[c]	NA
14	9	10	300	3600	6600	ND	0	300	0	0	0	0	0	0	ALL	O
15	10	8	400	5000	9000	300	0	400	0	0	0	0	0	0	A[e]	NA
16	10	10	0	7500	7500	ND	0	0	0	1000[d]	0	0	0	0	ALL	O
17	13	11	300	4800	7800	300	300	300	0	0	0	0	0	0	VAR[e]	NA
18			400	10000	14400	400	400	400	0	0	0	0	0	0		NA

a – $20 for Executive Committee; $50 for other committees
b – $6,000 for Executive Committee; $1,000 for Audit and Compensation Committees
c – An amount estimated to reimburse for actual costs
d – Retainer, to chairmen of all committees
e – Varying flat amounts, depending on distance traveled

Miscellaneous Industrial Products

No.															
1	4	0	500	0	0	NC	0	0	0	0	0	0	ALL	NA
2	1	NR	0	2400	0	NC	0	0	0	0	0	0	ALL	NA
3	2	10	600	6000	6000	600	NC	NC	0	0	0	0	ALL	NA
4	3	4	250	1000	250	0	250	0	0	0	0	0	300	NA
5	3	NR	300	NR	NR	NC	0	300	NC	0	0	0	ALL	NA
6	3	6	300	2800	1000	NC	175[a]	300	NC	225[b] 200	0	0	ALL	NA
7	3	13	300	3900	0	200	100	0	0	200	150	1950	0	ALL	O

NA—Not applicable
NC—No such committee
ND—No outside directors serve
NE—No employee directors serve
NR—No response

S—Same as outside directors
T—Transportation expenses only
VAR—Amounts can vary

A—Flat amount
E—Expenses only
F—Fee
P—Payment made but amount not specified
R—Retainer

* Asset groups ($000,000) are:
1—Under 10
2—10 to 24
3—25 to 49
4—50 to 99
5—100 to 149
6—150 to 199
7—200 to 349
8—350 to 499
9—500 to 749
10—750 to 999
11—1 but under 2 billion
12—2 but under 3 billion
13—3 billion and over

Companies within any given asset group are in random order rather than in rank by size.

Table 3: COMPENSATION OF DIRECTORS
570 Manufacturing Companies – Continued

Miscellaneous Industrial Products – Continued

			Outside Directors								Employee Directors					
Company	Asset* Group	Regular Board Meetings Per Year	Regular Meeting Fee	Annual Retainer	Total Potential Annual Compensation for Regular Board Service	Fee, Executive Committee	Retainer, Executive Committee	Fee, Other Committees	Retainer, Other Committees	Compensation for Committee Chairmen If Higher	Regular Meeting Fee	Annual Retainer	Total Potential Annual Compensation for Regular Board Service	Committee Compensation	Meeting Expense Payment	Honorary Directors Payment
8	4	6	300	3600[c]	5400	300	0	300	0	0	0	0	0	0	ALL	NA
9	4	8	200	1500	3100	200	500	200	500	0	0	0	0	0	ALL	NA
10	4	5	0	5000	5000	100	0	100	0	0	0	0	0	0	ALL	NA
11	4	5	200	1200	2200	100	0	100	0	0	0	0	0	0	ALL	NA
12	4	NR	0	4000	4000	500[d]	0	500[d]	0	0	0	0	0	0	ALL T	NA
13	4	4	500	0	2000	NC	NC	500	0	0	0	0	0	0	ALL	NA
14	4	12	100	3000	4200	100	0	100	0	0	0	0	0	0	ALL	NA
15	4	5	300	2400	3900	NC	NC	300	0	0	0	0	0	0	ALL	NA
16	5	5	400	2500	4500	NC	NC	150	0	1000[e]	0	0	0	0	ALL	0
17	5	4	500	0	2000	0	200	0	0	0	0	0	0	0	ALL	0
18	6	10	500	2500	7500	500	NC	0	0	0	500	2500	7500	500	ALL T	NA
19	6	9	300	6000	8700	NC	3000	300	0	0	0	0	0	0	ALL	NA
20	7	7	250	6000	7750	250	0	250	0	0	250	0	1750	0	ALL	NA
21	7	10	400	2400	6400	0	0	0	0	0	0	0	0	0	ALL	NA
22	7	6	100	5000	5600	NC	NC	100	0	0	100	0	600	0	ALL	S
23	7	7	0	8000	8000	NC	NC	250	0	0	0	0	0	0	ALL	4000 R
24	7	5	250	2500	3750	250	0	250	0	0	0	0	0	0	ALL	NA
25	7	9	200	5000	6800	400	0	200	0	0	0	0	0	0	ALL	NA
26	7	11	100	3000	4100	200	0	200	0	2500[f]	0	0	0	0	ALL	100 F
27	8	5	0	10000	10000	NC	NC	250	0	0	0	0	0	NE	ALL	NA
28	8	12	300	5000	8600	ND	ND	300	0	0	0	0	0	0	ALL	NA
29	9	8	500	4000	8000	NC	NC	0	0	0	0	0	0	0	ALL	NA
30	10	5	400	8000	10000	400	0	400	0	0	0	0	0	0	ALL	S
31	11	11	0	10000	10000	600	0	400	0	0	0	0	0	0	ALL	NA
32	12	4	500	8000	10000	ND	ND	500	0	5000[g]	0	0	0	0	ALL	0

a – $150 for some committees
b – $225 for Audit and Salary Committee; $200 for four other committees
c – Additional $300 paid in any quarter in which director attends divisional review
d – $250 if committee meets on same day as board meeting
e – Audit and Compensation Committees
f – Audit and Pension Committees
g – Audit Committee

Widely Diversified, Conglomerate

Co.	Group	Size												
1	3	5	240	6000	7200	NC	NC	O	NR	0	0	0	0	ALL	NA
2	4	4	4200	4200	4200	ND	ND	NC	0	0	4200	4200	0	ALL	NA
3	4	5	350	0	1750	500b	0	NC	0	0	0	0	0	ALL	E
4	4	6	250a	1500a	3000	250b	0	0	0	0	0	0	0	ALL	NA
5	4	4	750	5000	3000	NC	NC	0	0	0	0	0	0	ALL	NA
6	4	4	250	3000	3000	NC	0	NC	0	0	0	0	NE	100	NA
7	4	12	250	0	6000	NC	250	0	0	0	0	0	0	ALL	S
8	4	4	600	0	1000	ND	NC	NC	0	0	0	0	0	ALL	NA
9	5	8	250	5000	4800	600	600	0	0	0	0	0	0	ALL	NA
10	6	6	200	2500	6000	NC	250	1000c	0	0	0	0	0	ALL	NA
11	6	6	200	3000	3700	200	200	0	0	0	0	0	0	ALL	E
12	7	7	200	3000	4400	200	200	1000d	20	0	80	0	0	ALL	20 F
13	7	7	20	1200	1280	20	20	0	0	0	0	0	0	ALL	NA
14	7	6	0	5000	5000	0	0	0	0	0	0	0	0	ALL	NA
15	8	5	0	4800	4800	0	0	0	0	0	0	0	0	ALL	S
16	8	12	200	6000	8400	200	200	0	0	200	2400	200	0	ALL	NA
17	8	12	400	5000	9800	400e	400e	0	0	0	0	0	0	ALL	NA
18	9	7	300	4000	6100	300	300	0	0	0	0	0	0	ALL	S
19	9	12	750	5000	14000	0	750	0	0	0	0	0	0	ALL	NA
20	9	6	200	11000	12200	12000	200	0	0	0	0	0	0	ALL	NA
21	9	6	0	5000f	5000f	ND	0	0	200	200	P	NR	0	ALL	11000 R
22	11	11	300	7500	10800	300	300	0	0	0	0	0	0	ALL	NA
23	11	6	0	8000	8000	ND	0	0	0	0	0	0	0	ALL	NA
24	11	4	300	8000	9200	300g	300g	0	0	0	0	0	0	ALL	NA
25	11	6	0	12000	12000	400h	400	0	0	0	0	0	0	VAR i	NA
26	12	10	500	5000	10000	500	500	0	0	0	0	0	0	ALL	NA
27	12	7	500	6000	9500	500	500	0	0	0	0	0	0	ALL	125 F
28	12	12	250	10000	13000	ND	ND	500j	1250k	0	0	0	0	T	7000 R
29	13	4	500	7000	9000	ND	500	1000	0	0	0	0	0	ALL	500 F

a – Not paid to three directors employed by majority shareholder
b – Not paid to one committee member employed by majority shareholder
c – Audit Committee
d – Executive Committee
e – $200 if committee meets on same day as board meeting
f – Compensation varies; one director receives this amount, another receives more, a third receives less
g – $150 if committee meets on same day as board meeting
h – This amount for one committee; $200 for another
i – Directors within driving distance receive unspecified flat amount; others receive all actual expenses
j – $1,000 for Finance Committee; $500 all other committees
k – Finance Committee

NA—Not applicable	A—Flat amount	S—Same as outside directors
NC—No such committee	E—Expenses only	T—Transportation expenses only
ND—No outside directors serve	F—Fee	VAR—Amounts can vary
NE—No employee directors serve	P—Payment made but amount not specified	
NR—No response	R—Retainer	

*Asset groups ($000,000) are:

1—Under 10	6—150 to 199	11—1 but under 2 billion
2—10 to 24	7—200 to 349	12—2 but under 3 billion
3—25 to 49	8—350 to 499	13—3 billion and over
4—50 to 99	9—500 to 749	
5—100 to 149	10—750 to 999	

Companies within any given asset group are in random order rather than in rank by size.

Nonmanufacturing Companies

All but one of 414 reporting nonmanufacturing companies pay nonemployees for board service in the forms and amounts described below.

Forms of Compensation

As with manufacturing companies, payment of both a retainer and a per-meeting fee to outside directors remains a majority practice among participating nonmanufacturing companies (see Table 4).

Table 4: Forms of Compensation to Outside Directors in 413 Nonmanufacturing Companies

Forms of Compensation	Percent of Companies Reporting	
	1975	1972
Both retainer and fee	61%	59%
Retainer only	19	15
Fee only	20	26
	100%	100%

The retainer has continued to gain favor with nonmanufacturing firms, as it has also with manufacturing companies.

Amounts of Compensation

Chart 1 and Charts 4 through 7 (on pp. 3, 6, 33 and 34) show data on the level of compensation to outside directors of nonmanufacturing companies. On the whole, nonmanufacturing companies in the report pay less than manufacturing companies, which has also been the case in the past. The close correlation of compensation and corporate size that prevails among manufacturing companies (see Chart 2, page 4) is not found in nonmanufacturing firms, as Chart 6 indicates.

For data on directors' compensation in individual nonmanufacturing companies, grouped by industry, see Table 5 beginning on page 36.

Increases of Compensation

Increases in directors' compensation among nonmanufacturing companies since 1972 are erratic, like those in manufacturing (see page 7). For holding and investment companies (excluding bank holding companies), the increase in the median annual compensation figure for outside directors is about 11 percent, and for public utilities is 15 percent. However, for commercial banks the median annual payment figure is up 41 percent, and for service companies (financial and others combined), 43 percent. In the transportation industry, the median annual payment has more than doubled (a 115 percent increase). See Chart 7 on page 34 for medians and ranges for each nonmanufacturing industry.

Measured in terms of company size ranges, increases since 1972 vary considerably. The median annual compensation in nonmanufacturing companies

(*text continued on page 35*)

Chart 6: Annual Compensation of Outside Directors for Regular Board Service, by Company Size, 406 Nonmanufacturing Companies [1]

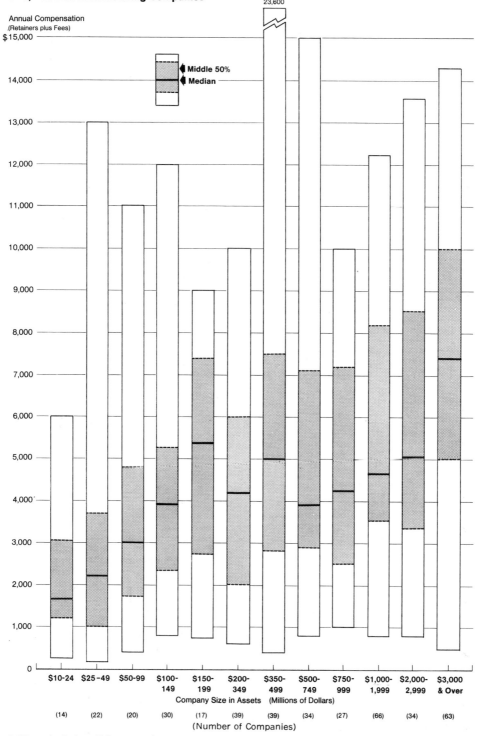

[1] Chart includes 405 companies; one additional company (with assets of under $10 million) pays $5,000.

33

Chart 7: Annual Compensation of Outside Directors for Regular Board Service, by Industry, 406 Nonmanufacturing Companies

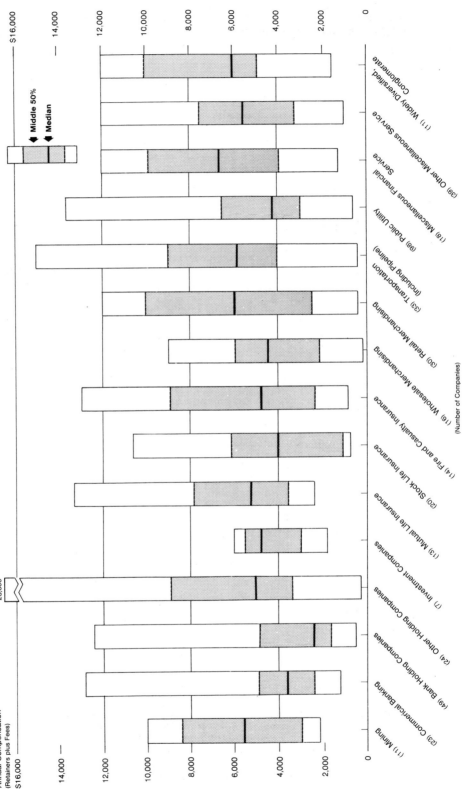

34

with assets of $50 to $99 million is $3,000, up 25 percent; in the $200 to $499 range the increase is 79 percent; in the largest companies ($1 billion and more), the increase is 16 percent. The smallest nonmanufacturing companies, those whose assets are less than $25 million, show a decrease of about 15 percent compared with the 1972 figure. Chart 6 gives more details on 1975 amounts.

Setting Compensation Levels

This report is organized so as to enable a company to compare its own compensation practices with other companies of similar size in its own or related industries. This organization reflects the fact that many companies are guided by the prevailing practice among their peers in establishing compensation levels for their directors. However, some companies use other approaches to directors' compensation, which are reflected in the figures in this report.

For example, the broad ranges in compensation in any given industry or size bracket show that some firms depart substantially from the norm. Reasons that have been advanced for paying directors better-than-average compensation include a conviction that their services and the risks involved merit it; a desire to be competitive enough to keep the services of valued directors and attract new ones; and the fact that in the company involved the directors make a greater contribution than is expected in a typical company.

An examination of Tables 3 and 5 (including footnotes) and a reading of section 4 of this report will show that a small number of companies distinguish among their outside directors and pay some more than others, to reflect a difference in the time spent or the role played by different board members.

Another approach used by some firms establishes compensation for directors on a basis at least roughly comparable to what their time is worth in their principal occupation, instead of using prevailing directors' compensation levels as the standard. This may be true of directors who have a consulting arrangement with the company, of course, but such an approach has also been used as a basis of compensation for regular directors.

It must be kept in mind that directors' compensation, like that of executives, can be subject to challenge from shareholders that it is "unreasonable." This serves as a constraint in setting compensation levels for directors, at least in publicly held corporations.

(text continued on page 54)

Table 5: COMPENSATION OF DIRECTORS
417 Nonmanufacturing Companies

Company	Asset* Group	Regular Board Meetings Per Year	Outside Directors — Regular Meeting Fee	Annual Retainer	Total Potential Annual Compensation for Regular Board Service	Fee, Executive Committee	Retainer, Executive Committee	Fee, Other Committees	Retainer, Other Committees	Compensation for Committee Chairmen If Higher	Employee Directors — Regular Meeting Fee	Annual Retainer	Total Potential Annual Compensation for Regular Board Service	Committee Compensation	Meeting Expense Payment	Honorary Directors Payment
Mining																
1	2	10	200	1000	3000	NC	NC	0	0	0	200	1000	3000	NE	ALL	NA
2	4	11	200	300	2500	NC	NC	NC	NC	NC	0	P	P	NC	ALL	S
3	4	4	250	2000	3000	250	0	250	0	0	0	0	0	0	ALL	NA
4	7	6	400	6000	8400	400	0	300	0	0	0	0	0	0	ALL	NA
5	8	12	500	1500	7500	500	0	500	0	0	0	0	0	0	ALL	0
6	8	10	300	5400	8400	300	0	300	0	0	0	0	0	0	ALL	NA
7	8	8	500	0	4000	500	0	500	0	0	500	0	4000	500[a]	ALL	S
8	9	11	200[b]	0	2200	200[b]	5000	200[b]	0	0	0	0	0	0	ALL	NA
9	10	7	300	3500	5600	300	2000	300	0	0	300	0	2100	300	ALL	NA
10	10	10	0	10000	10000	NC	NC	0	0	0	0	0	0	0	ALL	NA
11	10	5	500	6000	8500	500	0	500	0	0	0	0	0	0	ALL	NA
Commercial Banking																
1	5	12	100	300	1500	50	0	50	0	0	100	0	1200	0	0	NA
2	5	12	100	0	1200	100	0	100	0	0	0	0	0	0	0	NA
3	7	12	100	0	1200	25	0	25	0	0	0	0	0	0	0	S
4	9	13	200	1000	3600	200	0	150	0	0	200	0	2400	0	0	NA
5	9	12	200	2000	4400	200	0	200	0	0	250	0	3000	0	ALL	NA
6	9	12	250	0	3000	150	0	150	1200[a]	0	0	0	0	0	0	S
7	10	13	150	1200	3150	150	0	150	0	0	0	0	0	0	0	150 F
8	10	12	150	0	1800	150	0	150	0	0	0	0	0	0	ALL	0
9	10	12	0	4000	4000	NC	NC	300[b]	0	0	0	0	0	NE	T	200 F
10	10	12	200	0	2400	100	0	100	0	0	200	0	2400	100	ALL	S
11	11	12	100	1200	2400	100	0	100	0	0	0	0	0	0	ALL[c]	100 F
12	11	12	200	1200	3600	200	0	200	0	0	0	0	0	0	0	200 F
13	11	13	200	0	2600	200	0	200	0	300[d]	0	0	0	0	T	S
14	11	12	200	0	2400	150	0	P	300	500[e]	0	0	0	0	S	S

a – Executive Committee
b – Plus $200 extra to "nonresident" directors; extra fee not paid for committee meetings held on same day as board meetings

No.	Dir.	AG											Exp.		Type
15	11	12	150	1800	3600	150	0	12000^f	0	150	1800	150	T	NA	F
16	12	12	200	2500	4900	200	0	0	0	0	0	0	ALL	200	F
17	12	12	100	2400	3600	100	0	0	0	0	0	0	T	NA	
18	12	12	400	8000	12800	P	0	2500^d	0	0	0	0	ALL	400	F
19	13	13	200	7500	10100	NC	1500^g / 1000	0	0	0	0	0	ALL	NA	
20	12	13	200	5000	7400	200^h	0	7500^i	0	0	0	0	VAR^j	200	F
21	13	13	300	4000	7600	300	0	0	0	0	0	0	ALL	1000	R
22	13	13	300	4000	7900	300	0	0	0	0	0	0	ALL	300	F
23	12		200	1600	4000	200	2000^k	0	0	0	0	0	A	NA	

a – Directors Examining Committee
b – $150 if committee meets on same day as board meeting
c – If director's principal place of business is not in the county where bank is headquartered
d – Examining Committee
e – Auditing Committee
f – Executive Committee
g – $1,500 for Examining Committee; $1,000 for Compensation Committee
h – $300 for Auditing and Examining Committee
i – Auditing and Examining Committee
j – $85 for in-state residents, all actual expenses for out-of-state directors
k – Trust Committee

Bank Holding Companies

No.	Dir.	AG												Exp.		Type
1	6	12	100	500	1700	NC	NC	0	0	0	0	0	0	0	S	
2	7	5	200	0	1000	ND	ND	0	0	0	0	0	0	NA	NA	
3	9	13	200	0	2600	200	200	300^a	0	0	0	0	0	O	S	
4	10	13	100	1200	2500	100	100	0	0	0	0	0	0	ALL	NA	
5	11	4	250	0	1000	250	250	0	0	0	0	0	0	ALL	NA	
6	11	4	200	0	800	50	50	0	0	0	0	0	0	O	150	F
7	11	13	150	1800	3750	150	150	0	0	0	0	0	0	T	NA	
8	11	4	200	0	800	50	50	0	0	200	0	0	0	ALL	100	F
9	11	12	100	2000	3200	100	100	10000^b	0	0	200	0	0	T	NA	
10	11	12	250	0	3000	NC	250	0	100	0	1200	0	0	ALL	E	
11	11	4	200	1200	2000	100	100	0	0	0	0	0	0	ALL	200	F
12	11	12	200	1200	3600	200	200	0	0	0	0	0	0	O	600	R
13	11	12	0	4000^c	4000	50	50	0	0	0	0	0	0	O	0	

NA—Not applicable
NC—No such committee
ND—No outside directors serve
NE—No employee directors serve
NR—No response

A—Flat amount
E—Expenses only
F—Fee
P—Payment made but amount not specified
R—Retainer

S—Same as outside directors
T—Transportation expenses only
VAR—Amounts can vary

* Asset groups ($000,000) are:
1—Under 10
2—10 to 24
3—25 to 49
4—50 to 99
5—100 to 149
6—150 to 199
7—200 to 349
8—350 to 499
9—500 to 749
10—750 to 999
11—1 but under 2 billion
12—2 but under 3 billion
13—3 billion and over

Companies within any given asset group are in random order rather than in rank by size.

Table 5: COMPENSATION OF DIRECTORS
417 Nonmanufacturing Companies – Continued

Bank Holding Companies – Continued

Company	Asset* Group	Regular Board Meetings Per Year	Outside Directors								Employee Directors				Meeting Expense Payment	Honorary Directors Payment
			Regular Meeting Fee	Annual Retainer	Total Potential Annual Compensation for Regular Board Service	Fee, Executive Committee	Retainer, Executive Committee	Fee, Other Committees	Retainer, Other Committees	Compensation for Committee Chairmen If Higher	Regular Meeting Fee	Annual Retainer	Total Potential Annual Compensation for Regular Board Service	Committee Compensation		
14	11	12	200	0	2400	100	0	100	0	0	200	0	2400	0	ALL	S
15	11	5	200	0	1000	200	0	200	0	0	0	0	0	0	O	NA
16	11	12	200	1000	3400	NC	1200	NC	NC	1000[d]	100	0	800	NC	ALL	300 F
17	11	8	100	1200	2000	200	NC	NC	NC	NC	0	0	0	0	O	NA
18	11	4	0	2400	2400	100	0	150[e]	0	0	0	0	0	0	T	NA
19	11	12	150	0	1800	100	0	200	0	0	0	0	0	0	O	O
20	12	12	200	0	2400	200	0	200	0	0	0	0	0	0	ALL	NA
21	12	12	75	0	900	0	1800	0	600[a]	1000[f]/2400	75	0	900	0	ALL	S
22	12	7	300	1200	3300	200	0	100	0	0	300	0	2100	200	500	NA
23	12	7	500	1200	4700	500	0	100	0	0	0	0	0	0	ALL	50 F
24	12	12	100	0	1200	200	0	200	0	0	0	0	0	0	O	NA
25	12	5	200	1200	2200	200	0	150	0	0	0	0	0	0	VAR[g]	NA
26	12	12	150	0	1800	150	0	100	0	0	0	0	0	0	O	NA
27	12	12	100[h]	1200[i]	2400	100	0	100	0	0	0	0	0	0	ALL	S
28	12	6	400	1000	3400	400[j]	0	400[j]	0	0	0	0	0	0	ALL	NA
29	13	8	250	3000	5000	250	0	250	0	0	0	0	0	0	O	NA
30	13	5	200	4000	5000	0	0	NC	0	0	NE	NE	NE	NE	T	NA
31	13	4	0	1000	1000	100	0	100	0	0	0	0	0	0	ALL	E S
32	13	5	100[k]	0	500	100	0	100	0	0	0	0	0	0	T	S
33	13	5	200	3000	4000	200	0	200	0	0	0	0	0	0	VAR[l]	NA
34	13	5	300	7500	9000	300	0	300	0	5000[a]	0	0	0	0	ALL	2500 R
35	13	12	200	10000	12400	300	0	300	0	0	0	0	0	0	ALL	NA
36	13	4	250	0	1000	100	0	100	0	0	0	0	0	0	T	S
37	13	12	200	5000	7400	200	0	200	0	3000[a]	0	0	0	0	ALL	NA
38	13	10	600	6000	12000	200	0	200	3000	6000[a]	0	0	0	0	ALL	NA
39	13	5	500	6000	8500	250	0	250	0	0	500	6000	8500	0	ALL	NA
40	13	5	300	5000	6500	300	0	300	0	7500[m]	0	0	0	0	ALL	5000 R
41	13	4	350	1000	2400	NC	3500	150	0	0	0	0	0	0	ALL	O
42	13	11	150	5000	6650	NC	NC	150	0	0	0	0	0	0	ALL	NA
43	13	5	250	4000	5250	250	0	250	0	0	0	0	0	0	ALL	NA
44	13	8	200	0	1600	100[n]	0	100	0	0	0	0	0	0	ALL	NA
45	13	12	250	4000	7000	250	0	250	0	4000[o]	0	0	0	0	ALL	NA
46	13	11	200	5000	7200	200[p]	0	200[p]	0	0	0	0	0	0	ALL	200 F

No.														
47	13	13	200	600	3200	125	0	100q	0	0	0	0	0	0	NA
48	13	12	0	2000	2000	200	0	200	0	0	0	0	0	ALL	NA
49	13	4	200	0	800	200	0	200	500a	0	0	0	0	ALL	300 F
50	13	4	300	1200	2400	300	0	300	0	0	0	0	0	ALL	NA

a – Audit Committee (Examining Committee)
b – Executive Committee and Trust Department
c – Paid for joint membership on holding company and bank boards
d – Examining and Audit Committee
e – $100 for some committees
f – $1,000 for Audit Committee; $2,400 for Executive Committee
g – Actual expenses or flat amount, depending on distance traveled and means of transportation
h – Plus $200 if director also sits on board of subsidiary bank
i – Plus $1,200 if director also sits on board of subsidiary bank
j – $200 if committee meets on same day as board meeting
k – Plus $200 for subsidiary bank board meeting, held same day
l – Varying flat amounts are paid depending on distance traveled and need for accommodations
m – Executive Compensation Committee
n – $200 for some committees
o – Executive Committee
p – $100 if committee meets on same day as board meeting
q – Depends on committee; fees are $50, $100, and $125

Other Holding Companies

No.	Asset	Dir.												
1	2	3	75	0	225	0	0	0	0	0	0	0	0	NA
2	3	5	0	10000	10000	0	0	0	0	0	0	0	ALL	NA
3	4	10	0	3600	3600	200	200	0	0	0	0	0	ALL	NA
4	6	5	500	6000	8500	0	0	0	0	0	0	0	ALL	NA
5	6	4	250	5000	6000	50	0	3000	0	0	0	0	ALL	NA
6	7	12		5000	5000	0	0	1000	0	0	0	0	ALL	NA
7	7	12	200	2400	4800	100	100	0	0	0	0	0	ALL	NA
8	8	13	400	0	1600	NC	NR	NR	0	0	0	0	0	NA
9	8	6	150	3500	5450	NC	150	NR	0	0	5450	0	ALL	NA
10	8	6	600	20000a	23600	NC	150	0	150	3500	0	NE	ALL	NA
11	9	5	200	3000	4000	0	200	0	0	0	0	NE	50	NA
12	9	4	250	0	1000	0	250	250	0	0	0	0	ALL	NA
13	9	4	350	0	1400	0	300	500	1000b	0	0	0	ALL	NA

NA—Not applicable
NC—No such committee
ND—No outside directors serve
NE—No employee directors serve
NR—No response

A—Flat amount
E—Expenses only
F—Fee
P—Payment made but amount not specified
R—Retainer

S—Same as outside directors
T—Transportation expenses only
VAR—Amounts can vary

* Asset groups ($000,000) are:
1—Under 10
2—10 to 24
3—25 to 49
4—50 to 99
5—100 to 149
6—150 to 199
7—200 to 349
8—350 to 499
9—500 to 749
10—750 to 999
11—1 but under 2 billion
12—2 but under 3 billion
13—3 billion and over

Companies within any given asset group are in random order rather than in rank by size.

Table 5: COMPENSATION OF DIRECTORS
417 Nonmanufacturing Companies – Continued

Other Holding Companies - Continued

Company	Asset* Group	Regular Board Meetings Per Year	Regular Meeting Fee	Annual Retainer	Total Potential Annual Compensation for Regular Board Service	Fee, Executive Committee	Retainer, Executive Committee	Fee, Other Committees	Retainer, Other Committees	Compensation for Committee Chairmen If Higher	Regular Meeting Fee	Annual Retainer	Total Potential Annual Compensation for Regular Board Service	Committee Compensation	Meeting Expense Payment	Honorary Directors Payment
					Outside Directors						Employee Directors					
14	9	5	300	3600	5100	300	0	300	0	0	0	0	0	0	ALL	200 F
15	10	4	0	2500	2500	ND	ND	0	0	0	0	0	0	0	ALL	NA
16	11	4	250	3500	4500	250	0	250	0	0	250	3500	4500	250	T	NA
17	11	7	0	4500	4500	0	0	0	0	0	0	0	0	0	ALL	NA
18	11	8	500	5000	9000	500[c]	0	500[c]	0	0	0	0	0	0	ALL	NA
19	11	4	200	2500	3300	0	1800	200	0	0	0	0	0	0	ALL	S
20	11	12	0	12000	12000	NC	NC-	0	0	0	0	0	0	NE	ALL	NA
21	12	12	300	3600	7200	300	0	300	0	0	0	0	0	0	ALL	NA
22	12	4	1000	7200	11200	500	0	500	0	0	0	0	0	0	ALL	S
23	13	12	150	12500	14300	NC	NC	100	0	0	0	0	0	0	ALL	400 F
24	13	13	150	5000	6800	150	0	0	2000	0	150	0	1800	150	VAR[d]	NA

a – Maximum; retainers range as low as $3,500
b – Audit Committee
c – $250 if committee meets immediately before or after board meeting
d – First-class air fare plus flat amount for other expenses

Investment Companies

Company	Asset* Group	Regular Board Meetings Per Year	Regular Meeting Fee	Annual Retainer	Total Potential Annual Compensation for Regular Board Service	Fee, Executive Committee	Retainer, Executive Committee	Fee, Other Committees	Retainer, Other Committees	Compensation for Committee Chairmen If Higher	Regular Meeting Fee	Annual Retainer	Total Potential Annual Compensation for Regular Board Service	Committee Compensation	Meeting Expense Payment	Honorary Directors Payment
1	1	12	200	2600	5000	250	1500	0	1000	0	0	0	0	0	ALL	NA
2	2	11	0	1800	1800	NC	NC	0	NR	NR	0	0	0	0	ALL	NA
3	3	12	250	0	3000	NC	NC	NC	NC	NC	250	0	3000	NE	O	NA
4	4	12	0	3000	3000	NC	NC	0	NC	0	0	3000	3000	NC	VAR[a]	NA
5	7	12	500	0	6000	500	0	500	0	0	500	0	6000	500	ALL	NA
6	9	12	200	2400	4800	ND	ND	250	0	350[b]	0	0	0	0	ALL	NA
7	12	12	250	2500	5500	NC	NC	250	0	0	0	0	0	0	ALL	NA

a – All expenses, but only for meetings out of headquarters city
b – Per-meeting fee, Joint Committee on Portfolio Transactions

Mutual Life Insurance

#	Grp	Grp														
1	7	6	250	1200	2700	NC	NC	100[a]	0	500[b]	0	0	0	ALL	NA
2	7	12	150	600[c]	2400	150	0	150	150	0	0	0	0	O	S
3	9	4	200	1800	2600	200	1800	200	1800[d]	0	0	0	0	T	NR
4	10	NR	0	2400	2400	0	2400	100	0	0	0	0	0	T	250 F
5	11	12	250	1500	4500	250	0	250	0	0	0	0	0	ALL	NA
6	11	4	500	2400	4400	200	0	200	0	0	0	0	0	VAR[e]	S
7	11	7	300	2400	4500	300	0	300	0	0	0	0	0	T	NA
8	13	10	300	3600	6600	250[c]	0	250[f]	0	500[g]	0	0	0	T	NA
9	13	13	400	0	5200	NC	NC	300[h]	7200[i] / 2500	0	0	0	0	A	NA
10	13	12	300	5000	8600	300	0	300	0	0	0	0	0	ALL	NA
11	13	4	500	5000	7000	250	8000	500[j]	500[k]	600[l] / 600	0	0	0	ALL	NA
12	13	12	200	10000	12400	200	0	200	0	0	0	0	0	ALL	NA
13	13	11	200	4000	6200	NC	NC	200	9000[m]	15000[n]	0	0	0	O	NA
14	13	11	300	10000	13300	300	0	300	0	500[o]	0	0	0	ALL	NA

a – For all except Finance Committee, whose members receive $150
b – Audit Committee (annual retainer)
c – Board Chairman receives $6,000
d – Finance Committee
e – Per-diem payment (unspecified) plus 15 cents per mile
f – Ranges to $400 for some committees
g – Audit Committee, Committee on Corporate Responsibility and Public Issues (per-meeting fee)
h – $200 for some committees
i – $7,200 for Committee on Finance; $2,500 for other committees; alternate members of Committee on Finance receive $2,500
j – Organization and Operations of the Board Committee
k – Auditing Committee
l – $600 per-meeting fee for Organization and Operations of the Board Committee; $600 annual retainer for Auditing Committee
m – All committees other than Executive Committee
n – Committee on Finance
o – Per-meeting fee for all chairmen

Stock Life Insurance

#	Grp	Grp														
1	3	4	250[a]	1000	1000	0	0	100	0	0	0	0	0	ALL	NA
2	3	4	0	1500	1500	150[b]	0	150[b]	0	0	0	0	0	ALL	NA
3	4	5	200[c]	1000	1000	ND	ND	ND	ND	0	0	0	0	ALL	NA

NA–Not applicable
NC–No such committee
ND–No outside directors serve
NE–No employee directors serve
NR–No response

A–Flat amount
E–Expenses only
F–Fee
P–Payment made but amount not specified
R–Retainer

S–Same as outside directors
T–Transportation expenses only
VAR–Amounts can vary

* Asset groups ($000,000) are:

1–Under 10	6–150 to 199	11–1 but under 2 billion
2–10 to 24	7–200 to 349	12–2 but under 3 billion
3–25 to 49	8–350 to 499	13–3 billion and over
4–50 to 99	9–500 to 749	
5–100 to 149	10–750 to 999	

Companies within any given asset group are in random order rather than in rank by size.

Table 5: COMPENSATION OF DIRECTORS
417 Nonmanufacturing Companies – Continued

Stock Life Insurance - Continued

Company	Asset* Group	Regular Board Meetings Per Year	Outside Directors — Regular Meeting Fee	Annual Retainer	Total Potential Annual Compensation for Regular Board Service	Fee, Executive Committee	Retainer, Executive Committee	Fee, Other Committees	Retainer, Other Committees	Compensation for Committee Chairmen If Higher	Employee Directors — Regular Meeting Fee	Annual Retainer	Total Potential Annual Compensation for Regular Board Service	Committee Compensation	Meeting Expense Payment	Honorary Directors Payment
4	4	5	0	0	0	0	0	0	0	0	0	0	0	0	ALL	0
5	6	3	250	0	750	ND	ND	250	0	0	0	0	0	0	0	NA
6	7	12	100	0	1200	100	0	100	0	0	0	0	0	0	ALL	NA
7	8	4	400	0	1600	100	ND	100^d	0	0	0	0	0	0	ALL	S
8	8	4	500	6000	8000	ND	ND	0	ND	0	0	0	0	0	ALL	NA
9	9	4	500^e	0	2000	ND	ND	ND	ND	0	500	0	2000	0	ALL	300 F
10	10	4	250	0	1000	NR	NR	150	0	0	0	0	0	0	ALL	0
11	11	13	300	1500	5400	200	0	200	0	0	0	0	0	0	ALL	0
12	11	9	400	2500	6100	400	0	400^f	0	0	0	0	0	0	ALL	NA
13	11	4	250	3000	4000	0	9000	500^f	18000^g	0	0	0	0	0	ALL	NA
14	11	12	0	10000	10000	NC	NC	0	0	0	0	0	0	0	ALL	NA
15	12	6	200	2800	4000	200	200	200	0	0	0	0	0	NE	ALL 375^h	150 F
16	12	4	200	0	800	ND	ND	100^i	0	0	0	0	0	0	ALL	2400 R
17	12	4	500	3000	5000	ND	ND	200	0	0	500	0	2000	0	ALL	NA
18	13	4	0	6000	6000	NC	NC	100	0	0	0	0	0	0	ALL	S
19	13	12	300	7000	10600	300	2000	300	2000^g	350^j 24000	0	0	0	0	ALL	NA
20	13	11	250	5000	7750	NC	NC	250	0	0	0	0	0	0	T	250 F
21	13	8	0	5000	5000	0	2500	0	P	0	0	0	0	0	ALL	NA

a – $100 for any meeting director does not attend
b – For each meeting in excess of three
c – $500 for the annual meeting
d – Investment Committee members receive $100 per month rather than per meeting
e – $300 for any meeting director does not attend
f – Audit Committee
g – Finance Committee
h – Maximum: amounts vary according to distance traveled
i – $50 for some committees
j – $24,000 retainer for Executive Committee chairman, $350 per-meeting fee for most other committee chairmen

Fire and Casualty Insurance

#	Grp	Mtgs										
1	3	12	0	2400	0	0	0	0	0	0	ALL	NA
2	5	4	200	800	100	100a	0	1600	0	400	T	NA
3	7	4	400	1600	400	400	0	5000	400	0	T	E
4	8	4	400	5000	NC	Pb	0	3400	NE	NE	ALL	NA
5	8	5	200	3000	0	500	1000d	2500	5500	0	ALL	NA
6	9	5	600	5500	600	300	24000c	700e	5500	600	ALL	S
7	10	6	200	2200	0	4706	400f	21959	0	0	ALL	
8	11	12	200	2000	200	200g	7200h	1000	0	0	ALL	200 F
9	11	12	300	6000	ND	0	50000i	0	0	0	ALL	NA
10	11	4	556	10008	556	1668	12232	0	0	0	275j	1000 R
11	11	5	300	7000	300	1000	8500	1000k	0	0	ALL	NA
12	11	4	300	5000	200	0	6200	2000k	2500l	1200	ALL	200 F
13	13	11	500	7500	300m	5200	13000	2500n	0	0	ALL	NA
14	13	4	400	2000	400	600o	3600	500n	1600	1600	ALL	NA

a – $150 for Finance Committee
b – Retainer varies; amounts not specified
c – Executive Committee
d – Audit Committee
e – One committee only (not specified)
f – $400 per-meeting fee for Audit, Compensation, Investment Committees; $21,959 annual retainer for Executive Committee
g – Nominating Committee
h – $7,200 for Investment Committee; $1,000 for Auditing and Salary Committees
i – Finance Committee (annual retainer)
j – $350 if meeting lasts two days; out-of-town directors only
k – Finance Committee
l – Audit Committee (annual retainer)
m – $500 if committee meets on different day than board meeting; this does not apply to Finance Committee, which meets weekly
n – Audit and Executive Committees (per-meeting fee)
o – Compensation Committee; $400 for Audit Committee

Wholesale Merchandising

#	Grp	Mtgs										
1	2	12	100	1200	NC	NC	ND	NC	O	O	O	NC	NA
2	3	1	150	150	NC	NC	ND	NC	O	O	O	ALL	NA
3	3	5	500	2500	O	O	O	O	O	O	O	ALL	NA

NA – Not applicable
NC – No such committee
ND – No outside directors serve
NE – No employee directors serve
NR – No response

A – Flat amount
E – Expenses only
F – Fee
P – Payment made but amount not specified
R – Retainer

S – Same as outside directors
T – Transportation expenses only
VAR – Amounts can vary

*Asset groups ($000,000) are:

1 – Under 10	6 – 150 to 199	11 – 1 but under 2 billion
2 – 10 to 24	7 – 200 to 349	12 – 2 but under 3 billion
3 – 25 to 49	8 – 350 to 499	13 – 3 billion and over
4 – 50 to 99	9 – 500 to 749	
5 – 100 to 149	10 – 750 to 999	

Companies within any given asset group are in random order rather than in rank by size.

Table 5: COMPENSATION OF DIRECTORS
417 Nonmanufacturing Companies – Continued

Company	Asset* Group	Regular Board Meetings Per Year	Outside Directors: Regular Meeting Fee	Annual Retainer	Total Potential Annual Compensation for Regular Board Service	Fee, Executive Committee	Retainer, Executive Committee	Fee, Other Committees	Retainer, Other Committees	Compensation for Committee Chairmen If Higher	Employee Directors: Regular Meeting Fee	Annual Retainer	Total Potential Annual Compensation for Regular Board Service	Committee Compensation	Meeting Expense Payment	Honorary Directors Payment
Wholesale Merchandising – Continued																
4	3	5	350	0	1750	350	0	350ᵃ	0	0	0	0	0	0	ALL	NA
5	3	6	0	2400	2400	0	0	0	0	0	0	0	0	0	ALL	NA
6	4	4	250	1000	2000	100	0	100	0	0	0	0	0	0	ALL	NA
7	5	4	500	3000	5000	NC	NC	0	0	0	0	0	0	NE	ALL	O
8	5	9	250	3500	5750	ND	ND	0	0	0	250	3500	5750	0	ALL	NA
9	5	4	400	3600	5200	ND	ND	400	0	0	0	0	0	0	ALL	NA
10	5	4	200	3000	3800	ND	ND	250	0	0	0	0	0	0	ALL	S
11	5	6	0	6000	6000	0	0	0	0	0	0	0	0	0	ALL	NA
12	6	6	500	6000	9000	500	0	500	ND	0	0	0	0	0	ALL	O
13	7	4	ND	ND	ND	ND	ND	ND	ND	0	300	0	1200	0	NA	NA
14	7	12	0	6000	6000	425	0	425	0	0	0	0	0	0	ALL	O
15	7	5	100	3000	3500	NR	NR	0	0	0	0	0	0	0	ALL	S
16	9	6	0	6000	6000	300	0	300	0	0	0	0	0	0	0	O
17	10	7	400	3000	5800	400	0	300	0	400ᵇ	0	0	0	0	ALL	NA
Retail Merchandising																
1	3	5	0	3600	3600	ND	ND	0	0	0	0	0	0	0	ALL	NA
2	3	6	150ᵃ	0	900	150ᵃ	0	0	0	0	0	0	0	0	ALL	NA
3	3	5	200	0	1000	200	0	0	0	0	200	0	1000	0	T	NA
4	3	10	100	0	1000	100	0	100	0	0	0	0	0	0	ALL	NA
5	4	4	100	0	400	NC	NC	NC	NC	NC	0	0	0	NC	ALL	O
6	4	4	350	4000	5400	NC	NC	350	0	0	0	0	0	NE	T	S
7	5	12	100	0	1200	NC	NC	100	0	500ᵇ	0	0	0	0	T	S
8	5	11	200	0	2200	200	0	200	0	1500ᵈ	0	0	0	0	ALL	NA
9	5	NR	0	7500	7500	250ᶜ	0	250ᶜ	0	0	0	0	0	0	ALL	NA
10	6	7	625	1000	5375	ND	ND	275	0	0	0	0	0	275	ALL	NA
11	6	8	1000	4000	4000	100	0	100	0	0	0	0	0	0	T	NA
12	6	6	0	2500	2500	250	0	250	0	5000ᵉ	0	0	0	0	ALL	NA
13	7	4	0	2000	2000	0	0	0	0	0	0	0	0	0	ALL	NA
14	7	12	300	4000	7600	300	0	300	0	0	0	0	0	0	ALL	NA

a – Compensation Committee
b – Audit and Compensation Committees (per-meeting fees)

No.															
15	8	8	200	4800	6400	NC	NC	0	0	0	0	0	0	O	NA
16	8	8	1000	0	4000	NC	NC	0	0	0	0	0	0	ALL	NA
17	8	4	200	5000	7000	NC	NC	0	0	0	0	0	0	ALL	NA
18	8	10	0	5000	5000	NC	NC	0	0	0	0	0	0	ALL	NA
19	9	5	0	12000	12000	200	200	0	0	5000e	0	0	0	ALL	10000 R
20	9	12	0	10000	10000	ND	ND	0	0	0	0	0	0	ALL	NR
21	9	NR	400	3000	7800	400	200	0	0	0	0	0	0	ALL	1000 R
22	9	12	250	5000	8000	250	250	0	0	0	0	0	0	ALL	NA
23	10	12	300	7500	9300	0	200	2000	0	0	0	0	0	ALL	NA
24	11	8	0	10000	10000	300	0	0	0	0	0	0	0	ALL	NA
25	11	12	300	7500	11100	0	300	0	0	0	0	0	0	ALL	S
26	11	11	100	10000	11100	0	0	0	0	0	0	0	0	ALLg	1200 R
27	11	9	200	5000	6800	300	200	5000	10000f	0	0	NE	NE	ALL	NA
28	11	6	200	9000	10200	ND	200	0	0	0	0	0	0	ALL	0
30	12	12	300	1200	4800	300	300	0	0	0	0	0	0	ALL	NA
31	12	13	0	10000	10000	NC	NC	0	0	0	0	0	0	ALL	E
32	13	6	500	7500	10500h	500h	500h	0	0	0	250	1000	100a	325i	NA
	13	5	0	10000	10000	1000	1000	0	0	0	0	0	0		NA

a — Amounts of $125, $150, and (for board meetings) $200 are paid to various directors as per-diem compensation under consulting arrangements; one outside director receives no compensation
b — Executive Committee (per-meeting fee)
c — $500 if committee meets on different day than board meeting
d — Annual retainer, to all committee chairmen
e — Audit Committee
f — Advisory Committee
g — No payment to local directors when meeting in headquarters city
h — $200 if committee meets on same day as board meeting
i — For meetings in headquarters city; all actual expenses reimbursed for meetings at other locations

Transportation (Including Pipeline)

No.															
1	3	10	300	10000	13000	300	300	0	0	0	0	0	0	ALL	0
2	4	6	250	0	1500	NC	250	0	0	0	0	0	0	T	NA
3	5	12	250	1000	4000	NC	0	NE	NE	NE	NE	NE	NE	ALL	S
4	5	6	0	2400	2400	0	0	0	0	0	0	0	0	50	NA
5	5	4	200	1200	2000	200	200	0	0	0	0	0	0	ALL	S
6	6	12	ND	ND	ND	ND	ND	ND	0	0	0	0	0	NA	NA
7	6	6	500	3000	6000	250	250	0	0	0	0	1000	0	ALL	NA
8	7	4	250	0	1000	100	100	0	0	0	250	250	100a	ALL	S

NA—Not applicable
NC—No such committee
ND—No outside directors serve
NE—No employee directors serve
NR—No response

A—Flat amount
E—Expenses only
F—Fee
P—Payment made but amount not specified
R—Retainer

S—Same as outside directors
T—Transportation expenses only
VAR—Amounts can vary

* Asset groups ($000,000) are:

1—Under 10	6—150 to 199	11—1 but under 2 billion
2—10 to 24	7—200 to 349	12—2 but under 3 billion
3—25 to 49	8—350 to 499	13—3 billion and over
4—50 to 99	9—500 to 749	
5—100 to 149	10—750 to 999	

Companies within any given asset group are in random order rather than in rank by size.

Table 5: COMPENSATION OF DIRECTORS
417 Nonmanufacturing Companies – Continued

Transportation (Including Pipeline) – Continued

Company	Asset* Group	Regular Board Meetings Per Year	Outside — Regular Meeting Fee	Outside — Annual Retainer	Outside — Total Potential Annual Compensation for Regular Board Service	Outside — Fee, Executive Committee	Outside — Retainer, Executive Committee	Outside — Fee, Other Committees	Outside — Retainer, Other Committees	Outside — Compensation for Committee Chairmen If Higher	Employee — Regular Meeting Fee	Employee — Annual Retainer	Employee — Total Potential Annual Compensation for Regular Board Service	Employee — Committee Compensation	Meeting Expense Payment	Honorary Directors Payment
9	7	6	500	1200	4200	250[b]	0	250[b]	0	0	0	0	0	0	ALL	3200 R
10	7	12	0	4000	4000	0	1800	0	0	0	0	4000	4000	0	ALL	NA
11	7	10	0	10000	10000	ND	ND	0	0	0	0	10000	10000	0	ALL	NA
12	8	4	250	0	1000	100	0	100	0	0	250	0	1000	100[c]	ALL	S
13	8	4	100	0	400	0	0	NC	NC	0	0	0	0	0	ALL	NA
14	8	9	250	3000	5250	100	0	100	0	0	250	0	2250	0	ALL	NA
15	8	12	250	6000	9000	NC	NC	0	2500	0	0	0	0	0	ALL	NA
16	8	10	0	7500	7500	0	0	0	0	0	0	0	0	0	ALL	0
17	8	4	0	5000	5000	0	0	0	0	0	0	0	0	0	ALL	NA
18	9	9	0	15000	15000	ND	ND	0	0	0	0	0	0	0	ALL	NA
19	9	4	100	1200	1600	100	0	100	0	0	0	0	0	0	ALL	NA
20	10	4	500	6000	8000	NC	NC	0	0	200[d]	0	0	0	0	ALL	NA
21	11	4	200	4800	5600	200	0	200	1200[e]	0	200	0	800	200[d]	ALL	NA
22	11	11	200	3000	5200	200	0	100	0	0	0	0	0	0	ALL	O
23	11	12	100	0	1200	100	0	100	0	0	100	0	1200	100[d]	ALL	S
24	11	11	ND	ND	ND	ND	ND	ND	ND	0	300	0	3300	0	NA	NA
25	11	4	200	5000	5800	300	0	200	ND	300[f]	0	0	0	0	ALL	500 R
26	11	4	200	3600	4400	200	1200	200	1200[g]	20000	200	0	800	200[d]	ALL	NA
27	11	8	250	6000	8000	250	0	250	0	12000[h]	0	0	0	0	ALL	NA
28	11	11	300	7500	10800	300	0	300	3000	0	0	0	0	0	ALL	NA
29	11	7	300	6000	8100	300	3000	300	3000	0	0	0	0	0	ALL	NA
30	12	10	300	6000	9000	300	0	300	0	0	0	0	0	0	ALL	S
31	12	11	300	1800	5100	300	0	300	0	0	300	1800	5100	300[a]	ALL	NA
32	12	10	0	12000	12000	250	0	250	0	0	0	12000	12000	250[a]	ALL	NA
33	12	12	500	5000	11000	NC	NC	500	0	0	200	0	2400	0	ALL	NA
34	12	10	350	5000	8500	350	8500	350	0	0	0	0	0	0	0	1000 R
35	12	10	300	3000[i]	6000	300	0	300	0	0	300	0	3000	300[a]	ALL	NR
36	13	8	250	10000	12000	250	0	250	0	0	0	0	0	0	ALL	NA

a – Executive Committee (per-meeting fee)
b – $500 if committee meets on day other than board meeting
c – Per-meeting fee, committees other than Executive Committee
d – Per-meeting fee

e — Finance Committee
f — $300 per-meeting fee for Audit, Compensation, Executive and Finance Committees; $20,000 annual retainer for Executive and Finance Committees only
g — One retainer paid even if director serves on more than one committee
h — Executive Committee
i — Retainer is actually a monthly one of $300

Public Utility

#	Grp												
1	4	200	600	1400	0	0	0	0	200	800	0	ALL	0
2	10	0	1200	1200	0	7000	0	200a	200	0	0	ALL	NA
3	5	100	1200	1700	100	0	0	0	0	0	0	ALL	NA
4	6	300	0	1800	300	0	0	0	50	300	50	ALL	NA
5	6	0	3600	3600	300	NC	0	0	0	0	0	ALL	NA
6	4	500	300	2300	500	0	NC	0	100	1200	NC	0	S
7	12	150	1800	1800	NC	NC	NC	NC	100	2600	50b	ALL	S
8	6	100	2000	2600	50	0	0	6000b	100	0	0	T c	NA
9	12	150	1200	3000	150	NC	0	200	0	0	0	ALL	NA
10	5	0	4200	4200	0	NC	0	0	0	2400	0	ALL	NA
11	5	200	3000	5400	200	0	0	0	200	0	200b	ALL	0
12	12	0	3600	3600	0	0	0	0	0	0	0	ALT	NA
13	NR	200	0	2400	500	0	0	500b	NE	2400	200b	ALT	0
14	12	100	2400	3500	NC	0	0	0	NE	NE	NE	ALT	NA
15	11	100	1200	2500	NC	500	0	0	100	1300	NE	T	0
16	13	0	3000	3000	NC	600	NC	NC	100	0	NC	0	NA
17	9	120	0	1320	100	0	0	NC	0	0	0	0	S
18	11	200	3600	4400	300	0	5100d	0	0	0	300	ALL	NR
19	4	100	6000	6000	100	0	0	0	100	1200	100	ALL	NA
20	8	100	4200	5400	300	NC	0	0	100	400	100b	ALL	NA
21	12	150	0	600	100	0	0	0	100	400	0	T c	NA
22	4	100	2500	2900	0	0	0	0	0	0	0	ALL	NA
23	4	0	3000	3000	50	0	0	0	0	0	0	ALL	NA
24	5	300	3600	5100	50	0	NC	0	0	0	0	ALL	0
25	5	200	8400	9400	100	0	0	0	200	1000	0	ALL	NA
26	11	100	1200	2300	0	5000	0	0	50	550	0	ALL	0
27	4	250	1200	2200	ND	ND	0	0	200	0	0	ALL	NA
28	7	200	2400	3200	100	NC	0	NC	0	800	100b	T	250 F
29	10	200	5000	7000	100e	1000	0	0	200	0	0	VARf	NA
30	5	200	0	1000	200	0	0	0	200	1000	0	ALL	NA
31	12	200	4000	6400	200	0	0	0	200	1000	0	ALL	NA

NA—Not applicable
NC—No such committee
ND—No outside directors serve
NE—No employee directors serve
NR—No response

A—Flat amount
E—Expenses only
F—Fee
P—Payment made but amount not specified
R—Retainer

S—Same as outside directors
T—Transportation expenses only
VAR—Amounts can vary

*Asset groups ($000,000) are:
1—Under 10
2—10 to 24
3—25 to 49
4—50 to 99
5—100 to 149
6—150 to 199
7—200 to 349
8—350 to 499
9—500 to 749
10—750 to 999
11—1 but under 2 billion
12—2 but under 3 billion
13—3 billion and over

Companies within any given asset group are in random order rather than in rank by size.

Table 5: COMPENSATION OF DIRECTORS
417 Nonmanufacturing Companies – Continued

Public Utility - Continued

Company	Asset* Group	Regular Board Meetings Per Year	Outside Directors — Regular Meeting Fee	Annual Retainer	Total Potential Annual Compensation for Regular Board Service	Fee, Executive Committee	Retainer, Executive Committee	Fee, Other Committees	Retainer, Other Committees	Compensation for Committee Chairmen If Higher	Employee Directors — Regular Meeting Fee	Annual Retainer	Total Potential Annual Compensation for Regular Board Service	Committee Compensation	Meeting Expense Payment	Honorary Directors Payment
32	8	11	150	2400	4050	150	0	150	0	0	0	2400	2400	0	T	0
33	8	4	100	1800	2200	100	0	100	0	0	100	0	400	0	ALL	NA
34	8	4	100	2400	2800	100	0	NC	NC	NR	20	0	80	20	ALL	NA
35	8	12	250	0	3000	250	0	250	0	0	500	0	0	0	O	NA
36	8	4	500	6000	8000	500	NC	500	0	0	500	6000	8000	500[b]	ALL	E
37	8	13	250	4000	7250	NC	0	250	0	34000[g]	0	0	0	0	ALL	NA
38	8	12	250	0	3000	250	0	250	0	1500	0	0	0	0	ALL	NA
39	8	5	0	2400	2400	0	1200	NC	NC	0	50	0	2400	1200	ALL	NA
40	8	13	50	1200	1850	ND	ND	NC	NC	0	0	0	650	NE	ALL	NA
41	8	7	100	1500	2200	NC	NC	0	0	0	0	0	0	0	ALL	100 F
42	8	6	200	4000	5200	NC	NC	200	0	0	0	0	0	NE	ALL	NA
43	9	13	150	3000	4950	NC	NC	100	0	0	0	0	0	0	ALL	NA
44	9	13	250	0	3250	NC	NC	100	0	0	0	0	0	NE	ALL	E
45	9	6	0	3000	3000	0	0	0	0	0	0	0	0	0	ALL	NA
46	9	4	200	0	800	200	0	200	0	0	50	0	200	0	T	NA
47	9	13	100	1800	3100	100	0	100	0	0	0	0	0	0	O	NA
48	9	12	150	2400	4200	150	0	150	0	10000[b]	150	0	3000	150	T	150 F
49	9	20	150	1800	4800	150	0	150	0	0	150	0	1800	NE	T	NA
50	9	12	200	1200	3600	NC	1200	150	0	0	0	0	0	0	O	S
51	9	4	0	2400	2400	0	0	NC	0	0	0	0	0	0	ALL	NA
52	9	14	250	0	3500	250	NC	250	NC	500[h]	250	0	3500	250	T	125 F
53	10	12	100	3600	3600	NC	NC	NC	0	NC	0	0	0	NC	ALL	NA
54	10	10	100	3000	4000	ND	ND	NC	NC	0	0	0	0	0	ALL	S
55	10	12	150	1800	3000	150	0	100	0	0	0	0	0	0	A[i]	NA
56	10	11	200	1200	2850	200[j]	0	150	0	0	0	0	0	0	A[i]	NA
57	10	9	300	5000	6800	200[j]	0	200[j]	0	0	0	0	0	NE	ALL	NA
58	10	12	150	3600	7200	300	0	300	0	0	0	0	0	0	ALL	NA
59	10	12	250	1800	3600	NC	0	100	0	0	0	0	0	NE	ALL	150 F
60	10	5	250	3000	4250	250	0	250	0	0	0	0	0	0	ALL	NA
61	10	12	0	6000	6000	300	0	300[k]	0	0	0	6000	6000	0	T	NA
62	10	11	250	3600	6350	200	0	200	0	0	0	0	0	0	ALL	200 F
63	10	9	0[l]	7200	7200	500	0	500	0	0	300	0	2700	250	ALL	S
64	11	11	100	2000	3100	50	0	50	0	7500[m]	100	2000	3100	0	ALL	NA
65	11	13	200	1800	4400	200	0	200	0	0	200	0	2600	200	O	NA

No.	Grp	N														
66	11	7	1000	4000	11000	NC	NC	500	O	O	O	O	O	NA	ALL	NA
67	11	12	200	3600	6000	O	150	O	O	O	O	O	O	O	ALL	O
68	11	13	100	3600	4900	NC	NC	NC	NC	NC	O	NC	NC	NC	ALL	S
69	11	10	0	4200	4200	O	100	100	O	O	O	O	O	O	ALL	NA
70	11	12	0	5200	5200	0	100	0	O	O	O	O	O	O	ALL	O
71	11	10	0	7500	7500	3500	0	3500	O	O	O	O	3500	O	ALL	NA
72	11	13	400	5000	5200	NC	NC	NC	O	O	O	O	O	O	ALL	O
73	11	11	200	2400	7200	NC	NC	400	O	O	O	O	O	O	ALL	O
74	11	12	200	4000	4800	200	NC	100	O	O	O	O	O	NE	ALL	NA
75	11	4	0	3000	4000	NC	NC	1000	O	O	O	O	1000	O	ALL	NA
76	11	4	200	4200	3800	NC	250	NR	O	O	O	O	NR	O	ALL	NA
77	11	13	200	1800	6800	200	200	1000a	O	O	O	O	1000a	O	O	NA
78	11	8	0	3600	1800	200	200	1800o	O	O	O	O	1800o	O	ALL	NA
79	11	12	0	3600	3600	NC	0	0	O	O	O	O	O	O	T	4000 R
80	12	11	200	5000	7200	200	NC	0	O	O	O	O	O	O	ALL	NA
81	12	12	300	10000	13600	300	300	300a	O	O	O	O	O	O	ALL	NA
82	12	10	700	3000	10000	600	600	600a	O	400	O	O	600p	O	ALL	NA
83	12	12	200	4800	7200	100	100	300	O	O	O	O	O	O	VAR	NA
84	12	4	100	4000	4400	ND	50	100	O	100	P	O	O	O	ALL	S
85	12	5	200	2400	3400	ND	200n	ND	O	O	O	O	O	200	VAR	NA
86	12	7	200	5000	6400	200	200n	200	O	1400	O	O	O	O	100q	NA
87	12	13	200	6000	8600	NC	200	1000	P	O	O	O	1000	O	ALL r	S
88	13	16	200	5000	8200	200	200	O	O	O	O	O	O	O	ALL r	NA
89	13	10	100	8400	9400	100	100	O	O	O	O	O	O	O	ALL	NA
90	13	13	200	4800	7400	200	200	O	O	O	O	O	O	O	O	NR
91	13	13	300	5000	8900	300	300	O	O	O	O	O	O	O	ALL	NA
92	13	13	250	5000	8000	250	200	O	O	O	O	O	O	O	ALL	S
93	13	5	300	3900	5400	NC	300	2000	O	O	O	O	2000	O	ALL	NA
94	13	10	0	10000	10000	NC	0	O	O	O	O	O	O	O	ALL	NA
95	13	10	300s	7200	10200	330s	300s	O	O	O	O	O	O	O	ALL	NA
96	13	12	200	3000	5400	NC	75t	O	O	O	O	O	O	NE	VAR u	NA
97	13	12	200	5000	7400	NC	200	O	O	O	O	O	O	O	ALL	NA
98	13	12	200	3000	5400	NC	ND	ND	O	O	O	O	ND	NE	O	NA
99	13	12	150	2700	4500	NC	O	NR	O	O	O	O	NR	O	ALL	S

a – Audit Committee
b – Executive Committee
c – For directors who travel from out of state to attend
d – Audit and Executive Committees
e – $200 if committee meets on different day than board meeting
f – Varying flat amounts based on travel and reasonable expenses

NA—Not applicable	A—Flat amount	S—Same as outside directors
NC—No such committee	E—Expenses only	T—Transportation expenses only
ND—No outside directors serve	F—Fee	VAR—Amounts can vary
NE—No employee directors serve	P—Payment made but amount not specified	
NR—No response	R—Retainer	

* Asset groups ($000,000) are:

1—Under 10	6—150 to 199	11—1 but under 2 billion
2—10 to 24	7—200 to 349	12—2 but under 3 billion
3—25 to 49	8—350 to 499	13—3 billion and over
4—50 to 99	9—500 to 749	
5—100 to 149	10—750 to 999	

Companies within any given asset group are in random order rather than in rank by size.

Table 5: COMPENSATION OF DIRECTORS
417 Nonmanufacturing Companies – Continued

Company	Asset* Group	Regular Board Meetings Per Year	Outside Directors: Regular Meeting Fee	Annual Retainer	Total Potential Annual Compensation for Regular Board Service	Fee, Executive Committee	Retainer, Executive Committee	Fee, Other Committees	Retainer, Other Committees	Compensation for Committee Chairmen If Higher	Employee Directors: Regular Meeting Fee	Annual Retainer	Total Potential Annual Compensation for Regular Board Service	Committee Compensation	Meeting Expense Payment	Honorary Directors Payment
1	3	4	300	0	1200	100	0	0	500a	0	0	0	0	0	ALL	S
2	3	4	0	1200	1200	NC	NC	100	0	0	0	0	0	0	O	NA
3	4	9	250	2000	4250	250	NC	250	0	0	0	0	0	0	ALL	NA
4	4	4	250	10000	11000	NC	NC	ND	ND	0	0	0	0	0	ALL	NA
5	5	4	ND	ND	ND	ND	ND	ND	ND	ND	0	0	0	0	NA	NR
6	6	5	0	5000	5000	100	0	100	100	0	0	0	0	0	ALL	NA
7	7	10	225	5400	7650	Pb	Pb	225	Pb	Pb	0	0	0	0	ALL	NA
8	7	5	250	5000	6250	NC	NC	NC	NC	NC	0	0	0	NC	ALL	NA
9	7	4	250	1000	2000	250	1000	0	1000	4000c	0	0	0	0	VARd	NA
10	8	8	0	6000	6000	0	0	0	0	6000	200	0	1600	0	VARe	NA
11	8	4	100	2400	2800	100	0	100	0	0	0	0	0	0	ALL	NA
12	8	4	0	12000	12000	ND	ND	ND	ND	ND	0	0	0	0	ALL	NA
13	8	5	500	6000	8500	500	0	500	0	0	NE	NE	NE	NE	ALL	NA
14	8	12	350	4200	8400	ND	0	0	0	0	350	0	4200	0	ALL	NA
15	9	7	1000	0	7000	ND	ND	300	0	0	0	0	0	0	ALL	S

Public Utility - Continued

g – $34,000 for Audit and Finance Committees; $1,500 for Compensation and Succession Committee
h – Executive and Finance Committees (per-meeting fee)
i – $10 if director is local; $20 if from out of town
j – If two meetings are held on same day and last no longer than one-half day, only one fee is paid
k – $500 if meeting lasts for more than four hours
l – $600 per-meeting fee is paid only for out-of-state meetings
m – Executive Committee; paid as salary
n – $100 if committee meets on same day as board meeting
o – Paid (instead of per-meeting fees) for one committee only (unspecified)
p – Salary Committee
q – Not if director is a local resident
r – Only to directors who live more than 40 miles from meeting place and request reimbursement
s – $200 if more than one meeting is held on the same day
t – $150 if committee meets on different day than board meeting
u – Mileage allowance plus tolls

Miscellaneous Financial Service

16	11	12	400	5000	9800	300	0	0	2000^f / 500	0	0	0	0	ALL	E
17	13	4	1000	6000	10000	ND	ND	400^a	20000^g / 2500 / 750	0	0	0	0	ALL	NA
18	13	5	500	7500	10000	500	0	500	0	0	0	0	0	ALL	NA
19	13	7	200	3000	4400	200	0	200	10000^h / 7500	0	0	0	0	ALL	NA

a – Audit Committee
b – Retainers for members and chairmen of committees are by special arrangement; amounts not specified
c – $4,000 for Executive Committee; $6,000 for Senior Credit Committee
d – Non-U.S.-citizen directors receive $2,000 annual expense payment; all actual expenses of U.S. directors are reimbursed
e – Transportation expenses plus per-diem payment (amount not specified)
f – $2,000 for Audit Committee; $500 for Compensation and Stock Option Committees
g – $20,000 for Executive Committee; $2,500 for Audit Committee; $750 for Compensation and Stock Option Committees
h – $10,000 for Audit Committee; $7,500 for Compensation Committee

Other Miscellaneous Service

#	Grp	C														
1	2	5	500	0	2500	500	5000	500^a	2000^f	0	NR	P	0		ALL	S
2	2	4	500	0	2000	0	0	0	0	0	0	1000	0		ALL	NA
3	2	4	250	4000	5000	250	ND	250	0	250	0	0	0		ALL	NA
4	2	12	100	0	1200	ND	0	0	0^b	0	0	0	0		ALL	NA
5	2	4	250	0	1000	300	0	0	0	0	0	0	0		ALL	NA
6	2	4	300	2000	3200	150	2000	150	300^b	0	0	0	0		ALL	NA
7	3	4	100^c	1600	2000	0	100^c	100^c	10000^d	100	1600	2000	0		ALL	0
8	3	3	200	3600	4400	200	200	200	0	0	0	0	NE		ALL	NA
9	3	5	500	0	2500	500	NR	0	0	0	0	0	0		ALL	NA
10	3	4	0	1000	1000	100	NC	100	0	0	0	0	0		ALL	NA
11	3	5	500	3000	5500	NC	NC	0	0	0	0	0	0		ALL	NA
12	3	8	0	4000	4000	ND	ND	400	0	0	0	0	0		ALL	NA
13	4	6	400	1600	4000	NC	NC	0	NC	0	0	0	NC		VAR^e	NA
14	4	13	100	0	1300	NC	NC	0	NC	0	0	0	0		ALL	NA
15	4	4	0	6000	6000	0	6000	0	0	0	0	1000	0		ALL	NA
16	4	6	0	5000	6000	6000	5000	250	0	0	0	0	0		ALL	NA
17	5	6	250	5000	5000	0	ND	0	0	0	0	0	0		ALL	NA
18	5	10	0	12000	12000	250	ND	250	0	0	0	0	0		ALL	NA
19	5	4	0	8000	8000	ND	ND	0	NR	0	0	0	0		ALL	NA
20	5	11	200	3000	5200	NC	NC	200	0	0	0	0	0		ALL	NA

NA—Not applicable
NC—No such committee
ND—No outside directors serve
NE—No employee directors serve
NR—No response

A—Flat amount
E—Expenses only
F—Fee
P—Payment made but amount not specified
R—Retainer

S—Same as outside directors
T—Transportation expenses only
VAR—Amounts can vary

*Asset groups ($000,000) are:
1—Under 10
2—10 to 24
3—25 to 49
4—50 to 99
5—100 to 149
6—150 to 199
7—200 to 349
8—350 to 499
9—500 to 749
10—750 to 999
11—1 but under 2 billion
12—2 but under 3 billion
13—3 billion and over

Companies within any given asset group are in random order rather than in rank by size.

51

Table 5: COMPENSATION OF DIRECTORS
417 Nonmanufacturing Companies – Continued

Other Miscellaneous Service – Continued

Company	Asset* Group	Regular Board Meetings Per Year	Outside Directors — Regular Meeting Fee	Outside Directors — Annual Retainer	Outside Directors — Total Potential Annual Compensation for Regular Board Service	Outside Directors — Fee, Executive Committee	Outside Directors — Retainer, Executive Committee	Outside Directors — Fee, Other Committees	Outside Directors — Retainer, Other Committees	Outside Directors — Compensation for Committee Chairmen If Higher	Employee Directors — Regular Meeting Fee	Employee Directors — Annual Retainer	Employee Directors — Total Potential Annual Compensation for Regular Board Service	Employee Directors — Committee Compensation	Meeting Expense Payment	Honorary Directors Payment
21	5	4	1250	0	5000	100	0	100	0	0	1250	0	5000	0	ALL	NA
22	5	6	0	5000	5000	ND	0	0	0	0	0	0	0	0	ALL	NA
23	6	10	200	3600	5600	200	0	200	0	0	0	0	0	0	ALL	NA
24	6	4	200	7500	8300	200	ND	200	0	0	0	0	0	0	ALL	NA
25	6	8	100	7000	7800	100	0	100	0	0	0	0	0	0	0	NA
26	6	10	100	6000	7000	ND	ND	0	0	0	0	0	0	0	ALL	NA
27	7	4	400	0	1600	ND	ND	0	0	0	0	0	0	0	ALL	NA
28	7	4	50	6000	6200	ND	ND	0	0	0	50	0	200	0	0	NA
29	7	10	300	3000	6000	NC	NC	0	2500[f]	0	200	0	2000	NE	ALL	NA
30	7	5	0	6000	6000	ND	ND	250	0	0	0	0	0	0	ALL	NR
31	7	6	250	7500	9000	0	7500	0	0	[g]	0	0	0	0	ALL	E
32	8	4	250	4000	5000	0	0	500	0	0	0	0	0	0	ALL	NA
33	9	5	500	6000	8500	NC	NC	0	0	0	0	0	0	0	ALL	NA
34	9	6	100	10000[h]	10600	200	ND	0	10000	0	0	0	0	0	T	NA
35	9	12	200	5000	7400	ND	NC	0	0	0	0	0	0	0	ALL	NA
36	9	4	0	7500	7500	NC	0	0	0	0	0	0	0	0	T	500 F
37	10	6	400	5400	7800	NC	NC	300	0	0	400	0	2400	300	ALL	400 F
38	11	12	300	5000	8600	NC	NC	300	2500[i]	2500[j]	0	0	0	0	T	NA
39	12	4	250	5000	6000	NC	NC	250	0	0	0	0	0	NE	ALL	NA

a – Audit Committee
b – Option and Salary Committee
c – Fees are $100, $200, and $300, depending on distance traveled
d – Executive Committee
e – All expenses reimbursed for meetings not held at usual location
f – Some committees only (unspecified)
g – Office expenses of two committee chairmen are reimbursed
h – Paid only to one professional director
i – Finance Committee
j – Conflicts-of-Interest Committee

Widely Diversified, Conglomerate

No.	*	No. dir.													
1	2	12	6000	6000	NC	NC	0	0	0	0	0	0	NE	ALL	NA
2	2	4	1500	1500	0	0	NC	NC	0	0	0	0	P	O	NA
3	4	10	0	5000	ND	ND	0	0	NC	0	0	0	C	ALL	NA
4	5	5	2400	2400	NC	NC	NC	NC	0	0	2400	2400	NC	VAR^a	NA
5	5	4	10000	10000	5000	5000	0	0	0	0	5000	5000	5000	ALL	NA
6	5	4	4800	4800	0	7500	0	7200^b	0	0	0	0	O	ALL	O
7	7	12	500	6000	500	0	500	500	0	0	0	0	O	ALL	NA
8	9	4	0	12000	NC	NC	0	0	0	0	0	0	O	ALL	O
9	11	4	500	12000	500	500	500	500	0	0	0	0	O	ALL	500 F
10	13	12	250	9000	250	250	250	250	300	0	0	0	O	ALL	250 F
11	13	7	500	6000	0	3000	0	6000	0	0	0	0	O	ALL	4000 R S

a — Transportation plus $50 per day
b — Paid for service on both Audit and Compensation Committees

NA—Not applicable	A—Flat amount
NC—No such committee	E—Expenses only
ND—No outside directors serve	F—Fee
NE—No employee directors serve	P—Payment made but amount not specified
NR—No response	R—Retainer

S—Same as outside directors
T—Transportation expenses only
VAR—Amounts can vary

2. Compensation of Employee Directors for Regular Board Service

IT REMAINS A MINORITY PRACTICE to compensate employee directors specifically for their service on the board. Such compensation is slightly more prevalent among nonmanufacturing companies (86 of them, or about one-fifth, pay employee directors) than among manufacturing concerns, where the proportion is one-eighth. These ratios are essentially unchanged from those in the previous report.

The incidence of this practice in four nonmanufacturing industries is considerably higher than the 21 percent overall figure for such concerns. The four industries are: transportation (37 percent); fire and casualty insurance (but not life insurance) (36 percent); mining (also 36 percent); and public utilities (31 percent).

There is no significant correlation between company size and the payment of employee directors except for the very largest companies in the report, those with assets of $3 billion or more. Only six percent of such firms pay employee directors, compared with 16 percent of all companies combined.

The per-meeting fee is the usual form of compensation for employee directors: 118 of the 157 companies providing data pay only a fee; 17 pay both a fee and a retainer; and 22 pay only a retainer.

Table 6 shows fees paid to employee directors by 59 reporting manufacturing companies and indicates that slightly more than half of these companies pay either $100 or $200 per meeting, with $300 the third most common amount. Nonmanufacturing companies also favor either $100 or $200 fees for this purpose; see Table 7.

Retainers for employee directors paid by the 39 companies following this practice range between $200 and $12,000. The median amount is $2,500, and the middle 50 percent range is $1,950 to $4,850.

Table 6: Per-Meeting Fees to Employee Directors for Regular Board Service—
59 Manufacturing Companies

Asset Group (millions of dollars)	Number of Companies in Each Asset Group Paying Each Fee										
	$20	$50	$100	$150	$200	$250	$300	$400	$500	$600	Total
Under $25	..	1	3	..	1	..	..	..	..	..	5
$26-49	..	..	4	1	..	..	..	..	..	..	5
$50-99	..	1	4	..	..	1	1	1	1	1	10
$100-149	1	1	..	..	..	2	..	..	..	..	4
$150-199	..	..	2	..	2	1	1	..	1	..	7
$200-349	1	..	4	..	2	..	1	..	..	..	8
$350-499	..	..	..	1	2	..	1	..	..	..	4
$500-749	..	..	1	..	3	..	..	2	..	..	6
$750-999	..	..	1	..	..	..	1	..	..	..	2
$1,000-1,999	..	..	..	..	2	..	2	..	..	..	4
$2,000-2,999	..	..	2	..	..	..	..	..	..	..	2
$3,000 and over	..	..	..	..	..	..	..	..	2	..	2
Total	2	3	21	2	12	4	7	3	4	1	59

Table 7: Per-Meeting Fees to Employee Directors for Regular Board Service— 72 Nonmanufacturing Companies

Industry	Number of Companies in Each Industry Paying Each Fee												
	$20	$50	$75	$100	$150	$200	$250	$300	$350	$400	$500	$600	Total
Mining	..	..	..	..	..	1	..	1	..	..	1	..	3
Commercial Banking	..	..	..	1	1	2	1	..	..	..	..	..	5
Bank Holding Companies	..	..	1	2	..	1	..	1	..	..	1	..	6
Other Holding Companies	..	..	..	..	2	..	1	..	..	..	..	..	3
Investment Companies	..	..	..	..	..	..	1	..	..	..	1	..	2
Insurance (Life and Casualty)	..	..	..	..	..	..	..	1	..	3	2	1	7
Merchandising	..	..	..	..	..	1	1	1	..	..	..	..	3
Transportation	..	..	..	1	..	3	3	3	..	..	..	..	10
Public Utilities	1	4	..	9	2	7	1	1	..	..	1	..	26
Financial and Other Services	..	1	..	1	..	2	1	..	1	1	..	..	7
Total	1	5	1	14	5	17	9	8	1	4	6	1	72

3. Compensation for Service on Board Committees

THIS SECTION DEALS with compensation of outside and employee directors specifically for service on committees of the board—paid in addition to remuneration for regular board service. Figures for manufacturing and nonmanufacturing companies are not treated separately. However, compensation for executive committee service is presented separately from that for other board committees.

Payment for Executive Committee Service

Compensation of employee directors for service on executive committees remains a rare practice. On the other hand, five-sixths (518 out of 622) of companies with outside directors on such committees pay them per-meeting fees, annual retainers, or both for such service.

Table 7 contains information on compensation for executive committee service. The key figures in the table—those pertaining to outside directors—compare with the corresponding figures for 1972 as follows:

	1975	1972
Median fee, outside directors (executive committee)	$250	$175
Median retainer, outside directors (executive committee)	$2,500	$2,250

One-fourth of the companies that use a per-meeting fee to compensate directors for executive committee service do not pay the fee if the committee meets on the same day as a board meeting. A smaller number of companies reduce the committee fee (usually by half) under these circumstances.

Table 8: Compensation for Executive Committee Service

	To Employee Directors		To Outside Directors	
	No. of Companies	Percent[1]	No. of Companies	Percent[1]
Companies that pay per-meeting fees only	46	6.3%	424	68.2%
Companies that pay retainers only	3	0.4%	32	5.1%
Companies that pay both fees and retainers	(None)		62	10.0%
Per-meeting fees:				
Range	$20–$600		$20–$1,000	
Median	$200		$250	
Annual retainers:				
Range	$1,200–$5,000		$200–$18,167	
Median	$2,400		$2,500	

[1] Percentages based on 741 executive committees that have employee directors in their membership and 622 executive committees that have outside directors in their membership.

Payment for Other Committees

Compensating outside directors for service on committees other than an executive committee is common practice. Three-fourths of the companies that have such committees on which outside directors are members compensate them for this service, usually by means of an attendance fee. However, only 21 companies pay *employee* directors for service on such committees (see Table 9). The median per-meeting fee of $250 to outside directors for committee meetings is larger than that of $175 reported in 1972, although the range of such fees is essentially unchanged.

Most of the 687 companies that pay outside directors for service on committees other than the executive committee do so for each committee, but 56 of these firms pay only for some committees, not all. And some companies pay higher amounts for some committees than for others, as pointed out below.

As with the executive committee, some companies that would ordinarily pay a fee for a committee meeting do not do so if the committee meets on the same day as a board meeting. This is the practice in a fifth of the companies that otherwise pay for such service (for executive committees the comparable proportion is one-fourth), and there are also some firms that reduce, rather than eliminate, the fee for same-day meetings.

Table 9: Compensation for Service on Committees Other Than the Executive Committee

	To Employee Directors		To Outside Directors	
	No. of Companies	Percent[1]	No. of Companies	Percent[1]
Companies that pay per-meeting fees only for at least one committee	21	7.2%	591	64.7%
Companies that pay retainers only for committee service	(None)		42	4.6%
Companies that pay both fees and retainers	(None)		54	5.9%
Per-meeting fees:				
Range	$20–$500		$20–$1,000	
Median	$200		$250	

[1] Percentages based on 291 companies that have employee directors and 914 companies that have outside directors on their "other" committees.

A small proportion (14 percent) of the 687 companies that compensate outside directors for service on committees other than the executive committee use annual retainers for this purpose. Of the 96 companies that do use retainers, 55 pay the same retainer for all such committees. The range of the retainers in these 55 companies is $150-$10,000, and the median figure is $1,000.

The other 41 companies that pay retainers for committees other than the executive committee pay different amounts for service on different committees. Table 10 lists the committees and retainer amounts reported for them by these 41 companies. The median retainers for the three committees named most often by these companies—audit, finance, and executive compensation or salary and bonus committee—are identical to the 1972 medians for these committees.

Table 10: Incidence and Amounts of Annual Retainers to Outside Directors for Committee Service Other Than the Executive Committee[1]

Committee	No. of Companies Paying Retainer	Amount of Retainer
Audit	24	
Range of retainers		$250–$15,000
Median retainer		$1,000
Finance	16	
Range of retainers		$1,000–$21,000
Median retainer		$2,250
Executive Compensation/Salary and Bonus	15	
Range of retainers		$500–$15,000
Median retainer		$1,500
Investment	2	$2,500, $7,200
Stock Option	1	$2,500
Trust	1	$2,000
Public Policy/Social Responsibility	1	$8,000
Real Estate	1	$2,500
Planning	1	$1,200
Nominating/Membership	1	$800
Loan	1	$800
Share Unit	1	$800

[1] In 41 companies that pay different amounts for different board committees (other than the executive committee).

Table 11: Compensation of Committee Chairmen in 114 Companies That Pay Chairmen More Than Committee Members

Committee	Chairman Receives:	
	Higher or Special Retainer (No. of Mentions)	Higher or Special Fee (No. of Mentions)
Audit	58	26
Executive	42	12
Executive Compensation/ Salary and Bonus	29	20
Finance	17	4
Pension/Trust/ Investment	10	8
Stock Option	2	1
Nominating/Membership	3	–
Contributions	2	–
Organization/Operations	1	1
Environment/Safety	1	1

(Six other committees were mentioned once apiece.)

Extra Compensation for Committee Chairmen

One hundred and fourteen companies (12 percent of the total) pay some or all chairmen of board committees higher compensation than other members of those committees receive, or pay only the chairmen but not other committee members (designated as "special" in Table 11). The table shows that annual retainers are favored over per-meeting fees for compensating committee chairmen, especially for audit, executive and finance committees. Some companies report having a director who chairs more than one committee and who is paid one retainer to compensate him for this multiple responsibility rather than receiving separate smaller amounts.

Retainers paid to committee chairmen can be substantial. Amounts reported range from under $1,000 up to $90,000, with the vast majority falling between $1,500 and $20,000; the median is $4,500.

4. Other Compensation Practices

THIS SECTION PRESENTS INFORMATION that supplements the preceding material on basic compensation practices. It includes: reimbursement of the expenses outside directors incur in attending meetings of the full board or of committees; fringe benefits for outside directors; the use of deferred compensation arrangements; when compensation is actually paid; payment of fees for meetings not attended, or for electronically conducted meetings; compensation of special-status directors; indemnification and liability insurance coverage; and compensation of honorary directors.

Meeting Expense Reimbursement

Most companies pay at least some and usually all of the expenses incurred by outside directors who attend board and board committee meetings; 90 percent of the surveyed companies furnishing information on this point make such reimbursement. In a few cases expenses are paid only to directors who come from out of town or travel more than a stipulated distance to attend a meeting, or only for meetings held at locations other than corporate headquarters.

The following tabulation shows the principal approaches to meeting expense reimbursement, and the percentage of companies using each, among those firms that do pay such expenses.

Reimbursement Made	Percent of 876 Companies Offering
All actual expenses	87%
Transportation expenses only	6%
Flat payment	3%
Other; some combination of above, etc.	4%

The first two of these methods are self-explanatory. Principal varieties of the second two are spelled out below.

Reimbursement by Flat Amount

Among the companies that cover directors' meeting expenses by paying a flat amount, fourteen pay a single specified sum, as tabulated below:

Amount Paid Per Meeting	Number of Companies
$50	4
$100	2
$150	1
$200	1
$250	2
$300	2
$350	1
$500	1

60

Other companies vary the amount with the distance traveled to meetings. Five examples:

1. 15 cents per mile from each director's home office.
2. $25 or $50, depending on distance traveled.
3. $175 for 200 miles or less; $300 for over 200 miles.
4. 50 to 250 miles, $150; 250 to 500 miles, $240; over 500 miles, $350.
5. Payment according to distance as follows:

Miles	Amount
Under 50	$ 50
50-250	200
250-500	300
500-1,000	400
1,000-2,500	525
2,500 or more	750

Another variation is to scale the amount to the time spent on meetings. One firm gives its out-of-town directors $275 for a one-day meeting and $350 for a two-day meeting.

Other Reimbursement Methods

Some companies use a combination of methods to defray directors' meeting expenses:

• A combination of all actual expenses, transportation expenses, and flat amounts (e.g., $50 flat amount plus actual expenses in excess of that amount; round-trip, first-class air fare, plus $150 for outside directors living outside metropolitan area where company headquarters are situated; per diem plus 15 cents per mile).

• Different arrangements depending on where the meeting is held (e.g., a flat amount for a local meeting, actual expenses for out-of-town meetings).

• Different bases of reimbursement for different directors (e.g., in one firm, a flat amount for one outside director vs. actual expenses for other outside directors; in a second firm, $85 for directors resident in the corporation's home state vs. actual expenses for directors who live outside that state; in a third corporation, all actual expenses for the U.S. directors vs. $2,000 a year for foreign board members).

Benefit Plans for Outside Directors

Benefits of the type usually provided to corporate executives are not generally made available to outside directors, as Table 12 shows. Travel insurance is the most common benefit offered to nonemployee board members, but it is reported by only 17 percent of the companies this time, compared with 23 percent in 1972. The incidence of accidental death and dismemberment insurance, on the other hand, has increased from two to nine percent. Otherwise there are no significant changes since the earlier study.

There is little difference between manufacturing and nonmanufacturing companies in terms of the relative incidence of benefits to outside directors. Exceptions are group travel insurance and matching donations, which are somewhat more popular with manufacturing companies than with nonmanufacturing firms. (In the case of group travel, the frequency is 18 percent among manufacturers compared with 11 percent for nonmanufacturers; in the case of matching donations, 13 percent compared with 7 percent.

The usual approach to offering benefits to outside directors is to include the directors under the coverage of plans or programs made available to company employees. However, as the table indicates, some companies make arrangements specifically for their outside directors.

Table 12: Benefits for Outside Directors—969 Companies

Benefits	No. of Companies Mentioning	Per-cent	Type of Plan[1] Employee Plans	Type of Plan[1] Special Plans
Insurance:				
Group travel	162	17%	105	35
Accidental death and dismemberment	86	9	53	25
Group life	85	9	54	23
Group medical and hospitalization	36	4	29	1
Other benefits:				
Matching donations	101	10	70	2
Product or service purchase discount	11	1	–	–
Stock options	5	*	–	–
Pension	2	*	–	–
Assigned car	1	*	–	–
Club membership	1	*	–	–

Note: In addition, the following insurance benefits are offered by at least one company each: additional life, liability, automobile, home, dental, prescription drug, fiduciary responsibility under 1974 Employee Retirement Security Act, Workmen's Compensation.

[1] Totals are lower than total number of plans because some respondents did not classify plans.

* Less than 1%.

Deferred Payments for Directors

If a director's compensation can be deferred and paid to him at a future date when his income falls into a substantially lower tax bracket, he may gain a tax saving. But since the deferred compensation as a rule does not qualify for the maximum tax ceiling on earned income (currently 50 percent), a director is wise to consider the spread between his current and anticipated tax rates, the expected trend in the rate of inflation, and the tax ceiling on earned income before electing deferral. The year in which the deferred compensation is taxed depends on whether its payment has been funded or not, and whether it is forfeitable (e.g., should the director engage in a competitive business, as some plans provide).

The Treasury Department has set forth guidelines which make the tax deferrable until compensation is received if:

• The deferral is agreed to before the compensation is earned.

• The deferred amount is not unconditionally placed in trust or escrow.

• The promise to pay is merely a contractual obligation, not secured in any way by notes, etc.

If the deferred compensation has been funded, it is subject to tax in the first year that the director's rights to it become free of substantial risk of forfeiture.

The Treasury Department has ruled that interest credited to deferred compensation need not be subject to current tax to the director. It also sanctions deferred compensation plans that, instead of having the dollar amount of the fees or retainers payable in the future, calls for common shares of the company of equivalent value to be delivered in the future. As with dollar-deferral plans, the company may not set the shares aside in a trust or escrow account for the director. This would make them immediately taxable to him. He must have no interest in the stock until the shares are delivered, or the deferral will be destroyed.[1]

Ninety-seven firms included in this report, or 10 percent of the total, have deferred compensation plans for their directors. About two-thirds of these plans have been instituted since the beginning of 1970. In 1972, eight percent of the firms surveyed had such plans.

An analysis of plans, agreements, and board resolutions submitted by 47 firms reveals the following salient characteristics of these deferred compensation agreements:

• *The Director's Options.* It is, first of all, the option of the individual director whether or not compensation will be deferred. A slight majority (27) of the plans allow the director to determine what portion of his compensation will be deferred. Fifteen, however, require that he defer all of it or none; three permit him to defer both fees and retainers (all), retainers only, or none; one, all, 60 percent, or none; and one requires him to defer all, 50 percent, or none. And the director typically has the right to change his mind and switch back to current compensation in a later year. He must, however, exercise this opportunity before the period in question begins.

• *Memo Accounts.* Most of the full plans submitted either have specific disclaimers with respect to funding or assert that the deferred amounts will be held in the general funds of the corporation. But it is customary for the company to establish an individual memorandum or bookkeeping account for each director.

• *Forms of Compensation.* The most common arrangement is simply to credit this account with sums equal to the portion of the compensation that is to be deferred. These credited amounts draw interest as they accumulate. The rate may be fixed (the modal figure is six percent) but it is more common to establish a variable rate. The most popular is the prime rate on 90-day loans paid by a local commercial bank. Other examples: the rate paid by the company on

---

[1] Citations: Internal Revenue Code Sections 402; 403; 1348 Revenue Rulings 60-31 CB 1960-1, 174; 71-419, CB 1971-2, 220

short-term borrowings or on its most recently issued debt securities of intermediate term; the same rate as the company's incentive savings plan pays; for several banks, the rate paid on savings accounts.

To recognize the higher interest rates of recent years, one company amended its plan in 1971 with respect to interest to provide the following rates:

Deferred Compensation Earned	Interest Rate
Before 1970	5%
During 1970	7%
After January 1, 1971	Prime rate in effect at nearby bank on first day of each calendar quarter

Some plans are based on the company's common stock instead of cash. In these plans, sums credited to the director's account are used to purchase hypothetical or actual shares of company stock, and the cash equivalent of dividends on this stock is credited to the account, rather than interest. One company explains why it has adopted this type of plan: ". . . the company believes that the interest of the director in the company will be increased, and his compensation will bear a closer relationship to the value of his services, if the payment of his director's fees is tied to the value of the company's common stock."

Several plans offer a choice between simple deferred dollars-with interest, and stock-oriented compensation, or a combination of the two arrangements. And a very few provide several alternatives. For example:

". . . the company may, after consultation with director, either (1) hold such amounts as a cash reserve or (2) invest such amounts in the stock or other securities of any corporation or mutual fund. Uninvested funds shall accrue interest each year at the average of the prime rates in effect at the First National Bank of Chicago on January 2 and July 1 of such year, and the account shall be credited annually with interest earned based on the average of the month-end balances of such funds. . . ." Investment funds ". . . shall be credited with any gains on such investments (whether or not realized) [and] any dividends, interest, or other earnings on such investments . . ."

- *Disbursement Schedules.* Most plans fix the frequency with which—and the period over which—the director will be paid funds or other assets accumulated in his account once he retires or resigns his directorship. The most popular rate of disbursement is once a year; some plans, though, call for quarterly or monthly payments. Alternatively, a number of plans allow the director to choose between a single lump-sum payment or installment payments, or leave the determination to the company. With respect to the length of time over which disbursements are made, ten years or up to ten years are the most popular periods. Next is five years or less. As with frequency of payment, some plans give the director or the company options regarding this period.

A number of companies allow participants choices as to when they will start receiving benefits. A typical example: when the individual ceases being a director of the company, or when he retires from his principal occupation. The most flexible arrangement encountered permits a participant to begin drawing deferred benefits at any of the following times:

- When he ceases being a director
- When he ceases being an advisory director
- At age 65
- At age 70
- At age 72

If a director dies while in service, or after retirement but before all deferred benefits have been paid to him, his beneficiary or estate receives the funds due to him. Typically the beneficiary or estate is paid a lump sum. But some plans allow the company a choice as to the schedule of payments, and an equal number permit the director to set a schedule. The discretion may be absolute; or the company or director may choose from specified alternatives (e.g., the same schedule of payments the director would have attained had the director not died, or a lump sum). One plan stipulates that payments will follow the same schedule as if the director had lived, but his beneficiary can apply for a different schedule.

- *Other Provisions.* If the plan is discontinued—and quite a number stipulate that it may be discontinued at any time by vote of the board—the director is guaranteed to receive whatever sums have been credited to his account.

Suppose he changes his mind and wishes to have his compensation paid as earned: what about the deferred funds already credited? Some plans permit him to collect them at once. Others do not let him do so until he retires. Still others posit this restriction as a general rule, but allow for early payment of the accumulated funds if the director establishes that this would be justified by trying personal circumstances.

Most plans specify that a deferred account may not be encumbered or assigned (such a provision serves as another safeguard against the compensation's being regarded as current by the IRS). And there are penalties, in a number of plans, for a director who, without the company's consent, becomes associated, either before or after retirement (in one plan, only after retirement), with a competitive business. (In three plans, this is construed to mean, among other things, acquiring more than 10 percent of the common stock in a competing organization. In two, working for a government agency that has jurisdiction over the company or any of its subsidiaries is considered in the same light as working for a competitor.) Two quite different penalties are levied: either the director automatically forfeits the deferred compensation that he accumulated or that remains in his account, or he receives a lump-sum payment of this amount (which, of course, is likely to expose him to a heavy tax). One plan also requires that he reimburse the company for payments he has received prior to his association with the competitor.

How Fees and Retainers are Paid

Although a retainer is by definition an annual amount, only 52 companies pay retainers in a yearly lump sum. Most companies pay in either quarterly installments, which is the most common practice (461 companies, or 58 percent of those that use a retainer), or in monthly payments (29 percent). About five percent, or 42 companies, use a semiannual payment system. The remaining dozen or so firms report the following approaches to paying out retainers: every two weeks; at each meeting; and every two months.

Valid data for 1975 are not available on when fees are paid out. However, in 1972 the prevailing practice in two-thirds of the reporting companies was to pay fees at the conclusion of each meeting, while another fourth paid within 30 days following the meeting. Quarterly payments were made by six percent of the companies; a handful paid either annually or semiannually, or as requested by the director, or when the director submitted an expense report.

A small number of firms do make cash payments of fees at the meeting, rather than pay by check. In some of these cases only directors who request it receive cash, but in the others all directors receive cash fees at meetings.

Pay for Meetings Not Attended

Normally a director who misses a board or committee meeting forfeits any fee for that meeting. However, 23 companies report that they do pay a director a fee under certain circumstances, even though he is not present at a meeting. Among the 18 of these firms that explain the circumstances that would merit such payment, three simply pay absent directors as a matter of course. Seven companies make payment if there is a valid reason for the absence (reasons cited: the meeting is cancelled; the director must miss it because he is on other company business; weather or transportation conditions prevent his attendance; he has been excused). Five firms pay absent directors a fee if they have contributed advice or other input concerning matters dealt with at the meeting. And three companies reduce rather than eliminate the fee for meetings missed (from $250 to $100; from $300 to $150; from $500 to $300).

Some companies (in 1972, 11 percent of the respondents) make a practice of paying fees for meetings conducted by telephone conference call or other means of simultaneous communication.

Although annual retainers to directors are not usually linked to attendance requirements, a handful of study respondents say that if a director should miss an excessive number of meetings he would not receive his retainer (the practice in eight companies) or would receive a reduced amount (five companies).

Payments to Special-Status Directors

Respondents were asked whether the role or status of any *outside* directors on their board differed in specific ways from those of other nonemployee directors and, if so, what special compensation—if any—these special-status directors received. Since some of the information submitted on this point is subject to varying interpretations, a statistical presentation is only partially feasible.

"Officer of the Board" Or Similar Directors

Thirty companies have one or more outside directors whose status differs from that of other board members in a significant way, and who may bear a distinctive title—such as "Officer of the Board"—but more often, apparently, do not. In a few cases this special status is the result of a novel approach to board organization, but as a rule it is based on the distinctive role in the company of certain committee chairmanships or, less often, of the board chairman position (where the chairman is not chief executive officer).

In the five companies (all but one are public utilities) that cite the board chairman as an outside director with special status, the amounts of compensation given are:

- $34,000 per year plus meeting fees (chairman of the board is also chairman of audit and finance committees)
- $25,000 per year
- $16,000 per year, plus regular board retainer of $5,000
- $15,000 per year, plus regular board retainer of $3,000
- $12,000 per year, plus board fees

In some companies, outside directors holding certain committee chairmanships are described as having special status and are compensated accordingly. Some examples:

- Chairman of executive committee, $75,000 per year; chairman of compensation committee, $50,000; chairman of audit and directors committees, $20,000 (payment in each case covers all services in all capacities)
- Chairman of executive committee, $25,000 per year
- Chairman of executive committee, $7,500 plus part of his office expenses

Two companies have created highly unusual directorship positions, both tied in with early retirement policies governing top executives. In one firm, certain retiring executives have the option of continuing as outside board members with the title "director-officer." Such directors are expected to spend two-thirds of their time on board assignments, for which they are paid approximately two-thirds of their former executive salary. In the other company, certain outside directors (some of them retired corporate officers) bear the designation "general director." This position involves an obligation to spend a minimum of 30 days a year attending to board duties, but a general director may spend considerably more time than that, and his compensation is adjusted accordingly, as follows:

Days of Service Per Year	Annual Compensation
30 (minimum)	$30,000 (minimum)
40	$37,500
60	$52,500
80	$62,500

Also serving on the board of this same company are board members whose role is more like that of the typical outside director. Called "directors," they are expected to spend 15 days on their board responsibilities and receive $15,000 annually, plus $1,000 per day for extra committee work. A third category of director in this firm, called "officer of the board," is an officer-director whose compensation is in the form of salary but spends a majority of his time on board work.[1]

Here are compensation arrangements for special-status outside directors in some other companies that have such directors:

- $1,500 per month
- $300 per day plus travel expenses ("Officer of the Board")
- $200 per meeting ("Advisory Directors")

Director-Consultants

One hundred and seventy-nine companies (18 percent of the total) have outsiders on their boards who are being paid by the company for providing consulting services in addition to their normal board duties. This figure does *not* include the common situation in which an attorney is a director of a company that his law firm serves as outside counsel.

The information available on how the reported director-consultant arrangements work does not lend itself to the precision of statistics, but certain observations are possible:

- Some of the directors who have a paid consulting relationship with the companies on whose boards they serve are professional consultants (either independent or members of management consulting firms) or experts in a field such as investment banking, but it is also not unusual to find former officers of the corporation itself in the director-consultant role.

- In some cases the compensation for consulting services rendered is paid separately from regular director's remuneration, but in other firms the payment for consulting work also covers the director's services as a member of the board.

Professional Directors

Eighty-seven companies have on their boards one or more professional directors. A "professional director" is defined as someone for whom service on several corporate boards is his primary occupation or activity. In most cases these directors receive the same compensation as other outside directors with whom they serve, but ten firms report having a special compensation arrangement for their professional directors. The higher pay cited by these companies reflects an unusual role for the professional directors on these boards.

---

[1] For more detail on how these special board roles are delineated in these two companies, see *Corporate Directorship Practices: Role, Selection and Legal Status of the Board,* Report No. 646, 1975, pages 36-39.

One approach is to pay a retainer to professional directors in place of, or in addition to, the fee per meeting used to compensate other board members; or, if other directors receive a retainer, to pay the professional director a larger one. In several firms the extra compensation to the professional directors is described as a consulting fee, while in a few cases it is in recognition of special responsibility as a committee chairman. One professional director who chairs an audit committee is not paid additional compensation, but he is given a special reimbursement to cover office expenses connected with his chairman's duties. One company follows the unusual procedure of making a professional director eligible for a bonus based on profits and paid through key-executive incentive plans.

Indemnification and Liability Insurance

It is close to universal practice among responding companies to indemnify directors against losses sustained personally as a result of legal actions arising out of their activities as board members. Of the 975 companies offering information, 947, or 97 percent, provide this kind of protection for directors. This is a slightly higher percentage than in 1972 (94 percent).

An increasingly popular means of providing protection for directors and the company alike is a form of insurance known as "directors' and officers' liability insurance." Currently, 77 percent of the study participants (763 companies) carry it; the figure in 1972 was 62 percent. Of the companies that do have such insurance, 93 percent pay all of the premium, and another six percent pick up between 90 and 99 percent of the premium.

Limits of Coverage

Coverage limits reported for this insurance range from a low of $1 million (48 companies) up to $50 million (six companies). By far the most common coverage limits reported are $5 million (213 companies) and $10 million (237).

Table 13: Limits of Coverage for Directors' and Officers' Liability Insurance[1]

Limits of Coverage (in millions)	Number of Companies Overall	Number of Manufacturing Companies	Number of Nonmanufacturing Companies
$ 1.0	48	27	21
$ 1.5	5	3	2
$ 2.0	19	10	9
$ 3.0	35	16	19
$ 5.0	213	125	88
$10.0	237	152	85
$15.0	37	21	16
$20.0	76	37	39
$25.0	18	10	8
$30.0	5	3	2
$50.0	6	3	3
Total	699	407	292

[1] Only coverages reported by at least five companies are tabulated. Other coverages (in millions): $4.0 (3 companies), $7.5 (2 companies), $12.0 (2 companies), $35.0 (1 company), $40.0 (1 company).

> "Directors' and officers' liability insurance" denotes a specific form of protection that is usually written in two separate policies. One policy is designed to reimburse individual directors (and officers) for liabilities and expenses for which they are not indemnified by the company. The other policy covers the company for payments it may make to directors and officers under the company's indemnification provisions.
>
> It was once common practice for directors as individuals to assume a portion of the total premium for this type of insurance, since a part of the coverage applied to them directly. This is no longer so; over nine out of ten of the companies in this report that carry this form of insurance pay the entire premium. One reason for this may be that enabling legislation in popular states of incorporation, such as Delaware, permits corporations to do so.

The amounts of coverage reported in 1975 are generally higher than in 1972, when the maximum coverage reported was $30 million and $5 million was the median as well as the modal (most frequent) coverage.

Compensation of Honorary Directors

There are 269 companies that appoint or elect directors to honorary or emeritus status after their retirement from active board service. Just under 60 percent of the companies that have such directors pay them, but in half these cases the payment is a different amount—in all but one case, a smaller amount—than regular directors receive. The reason for the pay differential in many of these companies is that honorary directors do not receive the annual retainer paid to regular directors. In fact, the per-meeting fee is the most common method of paying honorary directors; 118 companies report paying a fee whereas 69 use a retainer. (Some pay both and appear in both counts.)

Table 14 gives a breakdown of compensation practices for honorary directors. Tables 3 and 5 include a company-by-company indication of forms of payment and amounts.

Table 14: Compensation Practices for Honorary Directors

	No. of Companies	Percent
No compensation	84	31.5%
Same compensation as active directors	78	29.2%
Different compensation from active directors	78	29.2%
Meeting expenses only	27	10.1%
Totals	267[1]	100.0%

[1] Two companies with honorary directors did not indicate their practice.

List of Participants

The following companies submitted information used in this report. Not listed are firms that cooperated in the survey but declined to be named as participants.

A. J. Industries, Inc.
AMP Incorporated
ARA Services, Inc.
Abbott Laboratories
Acme-Cleveland Corporation
Acme United Corp.
The Adams Express Company
Addressograph-Multigraph Corporation
Aetna Life and Casualty Company
After Six, Inc.
Aguirre Company
Air Products and Chemicals, Inc.
Akzona Incorporated
Alabama Gas Corporation
Albany International Corp.
Alberto-Culver Company
Albertson's, Inc.
Alexander & Alexander Services Inc.
Allegheny Airlines, Inc.
Allegheny Ludlum Industries, Inc.
Allied Chemical Corporation
Allied Stores Corporation
Allied Supermarkets, Inc.
Aluminum Company of America
Amax Inc.
Amcord, Inc.
Amerada Hess Corporation
American Airlines, Inc.
American Appraisal Associates, Inc.
American Bakeries Company
American Broadcasting Companies, Inc.
American Chain & Cable Company, Inc.
American Cyanamid Company
American District Telegraph Company
American Electronic Laboratories, Inc.
American General Insurance Company
American Home Products Corporation
American Hospital Supply Corporation
American Investment Company
American Motors Corporation
American Natural Gas Company
American Re-Insurance Company
American Security and Trust Company
American Smelting and Refining Company
American Standard, Inc.
American Stores Company
American United Life Insurance Co.
Ameron, Inc.

Ampex Corporation
Amstar Corporation
Amsted Industries Incorporated
The Anaconda Company
Anchor Coupling Co.
Anchor Hocking Corporation
Anderson, Clayton & Co.
Anheuser-Busch, Inc.
Anta Corporation
Apeco Corporation
Archon Pure Products Corporation
Arizona Public Service Company
Armstrong Cork Company
Associated Coca-Cola Bottling Co., Inc.
Associated Spring Corporation
Athlone Industries, Inc.
Atlantic City Electric Company
Avery Products Corporation
Avon Products, Inc.
Azcon Corporation
Aztec Oil & Gas Company
The Babcock & Wilcox Company
Bache Group Inc.
Baker Oil Tools, Inc.
Ball Corporation
BanCal Tri-State Corporation
Bangor Punta Corporation
Bank of America, N. T. & S. A.
The Bank of New York Company, Inc.
Bank of Virginia Company
Bankers Trust New York Corporation
Bankers Trust of South Carolina
Barnes Engineering Company
Basic Incorporated
Baxter Laboratories, Inc.
Becton, Dickinson and Company
The Bekins Company
Bell & Howell Company
The Bendix Corporation
Bergstrom Paper Company
Berkshire Life Insurance Co.
Bethlehem Steel Corporation
The Bibb Company
Binney & Smith Inc.
The Black & Decker Mfg. Co.
Blessings Corporation
Bliss & Laughlin Industries, Incorporated
Blue Bell, Inc.

Bluebird Incorporated
The Boelng Company
Bohemia Inc.
Boise Cascade Corporation
Borden, Inc.
Borg-Warner Corporation
The Boston Company, Inc.
Boston Edison Company
Bourns, Inc.
The Bovaird Supply Co.
Bowne & Co., Inc.
Braniff Airways, Incorporated
Braun Engineering Company
C. Brewer and Company, Limited
Briggs & Stratton Corporation
Brockway Glass Company, Inc.
The Brooklyn Union Gas Company
Bobbie Brooks, Incorporated
Brown Group, Inc.
Brown-Forman Distillers Corporation
Brown & Sharpe Manufacturing Company
Browning-Ferris Industries, Inc.
Bucyrus-Erie Company
Bulova Watch Company, Inc.
Bunker Ramo Corp.
Burlington Industries, Inc.
Burlington Northern Inc.
Burndy Corporation
Butler Manufacturing Company
CBS Inc.
CFS Continental, Inc.
C & K Petroleum, Inc.
CLC of America, Inc.
CNA Financial Corporation
CPC International Inc.
CRS Design Associates, Inc.
Cabot Corporation
California Computer Products, Inc.
California Life Corporation
California-Pacific Utilities Company
California Portland Cement Company
California Water Service Company
Calspan Corporation
Campbell Soup Company
Campbell Taggart, Inc.
Capitol Industries-EMI, Inc.
The Carborundum Company
Carlisle Corporation
Carolina Freight Carriers Corporation
Carolina Power & Light Company
Carpenter Technology Corporation
Carrier Corporation
Carter Hawley Hale Stores, Inc.
Cascade Natural Gas Corporation
Castle & Cooke, Inc.
Caterpillar Tractor Co.

Celina Financial Corporation
Centennial Corporation
Centex Corporation
Central Hudson Gas & Electric Corporation
Central Illinois Light Company
Central Penn National Bank
Central Securities Corporation
Central Soya Company, Inc.
Certain-teed Products Corporation
Champion International Corporation
Champion Spark Plug Company
The Chase Manhattan Corporation
Chemetron Corporation
Chemical New York Corporation
Chicago Pneumatic Tool Company
Chrysler Corporation
The Chubb Corporation
The Cincinnati Gas & Electric Co.
Cincinnati Milacron, Inc.
Citicorp
Cities Service Company
Clark Equipment Company
The Cleveland-Cliffs Iron Company
The Cleveland Electric Illuminating
  Company
Cluett, Peabody & Co., Inc.
Coca-Cola Bottling Company of
  Los Angeles
The Coca-Cola Bottling Company of
  New York, Inc.
The Coca-Cola Company
Coldwell, Banker & Company
College/University Corporation
Colonial Life & Accident Insurance
  Company
The Columbia Gas System, Inc.
Columbus and Southern Ohio Electric
  Company
Cominco Ltd.
Commercial Credit Company
Commercial Shearing, Inc.
Commonwealth Edison Company
Commonwealth Land Title Insurance
  Company
Commonwealth Oil Refining Company, Inc.
Communications Satellite Corporation
Computer Investors Group, Inc.
Computer Sciences Corporation
Condec Corporation
Cone Mills Corporation
The Connecticut Bank and Trust Company
Connecticut General Insurance Corporation
Connecticut Mutual Life Insurance
  Company
Connecticut Natural Gas Corporation
Conrac Corp.

Conrock Co.
Consolidated Edison Company of
New York, Inc.
Consolidated Freightways, Inc.
Consolidated Natural Gas Company
Consolidated Papers, Inc.
Consumers Power Company
Continental Air Lines, Inc.
Continental Bank
Continental Can Company, Inc.
The Continental Corporation
Continental Oil Company
Conwed Corporation
Cook United, Inc.
Cooper Industries, Inc.
Cooper Laboratories, Inc.
Corning Glass Works
Crane Co.
Crompton Company, Inc.
Crompton & Knowles Corp.
Crouse-Hinds Company
Crown Central Petroleum Corporation
Crown Zellerbach Corporation
Cullum Companies, Inc.
Cummins Engine Company, Inc.
Cunningham Drug Stores, Incorporated
Curtiss-Wright Corporation
Cutler-Hammer, Inc.
Cyclops Corporation
DPF Incorporated
Dana Corporation
Datapoint Corporation
Theo. H. Davies & Co., Ltd.
The Dayton Power and Light Company
Deere & Company
The De Laval Separator Company
Delaware Trust Company
Delmarva Power & Light Company
Del Monte Corporation
Delta Air Lines, Inc.
Dennison Manufacturing Company
The Detroit Edison Company
Diamond International Corporation
Diamond M Drilling Company
Diamond Shamrock Corporation
A. B. Dick Co.
Diebold, Incorporated
Di Giorgio Corporation
Dillon Companies, Inc.
Walt Disney Productions
Diversified Industries, Inc.
The Joseph Dixon Crucible Company
Donaldson Company, Inc.
R. R. Donnelley & Sons Company
Dorr-Oliver Incorporated
Ducommun Incorporated

E. I. du Pont de Nemours and Company
E-B Industries, Inc.
EG & G, Inc.
ESB Incorporated
Eagle-Picher Industries, Inc.
Easco Corporation
Eastern Gas & Fuel Associates
Eastmet Corporation
Eaton Corporation
Echlin Manufacturing Company
Edo Corporation
El Chico Corporation
The El Paso Company
El Paso Electric Company
Electric Hose & Rubber Co.
Elizabethtown Water Company
Elwell-Parker Electric Company
The Empire District Electric Company
Envirotech Corporation
Equimark Corporation
The Equitable Bancorporation
Equitable Gas Company
The Equitable Life Assurance Society of
the United States
The Equitable Life Mortgage and
Realty Investors
Equitable Savings & Loan Association
Equity Oil Company
Esmark, Inc.
Exxon Corporation
FMC Corporation
Fairchild Camera & Instrument Corp.
Fairmont Foods Company
Farah Manufacturing Company, Inc.
Farmers Group, Inc.
Fashion Fabrics, Inc.
Federal-Mogul Corporation
Federal Paper Board Company, Inc.
Federated Capital Corporation
FIDELCOR, Inc.
Fidelity Corporation
Fidelity and Deposit Company of Maryland
Fidelity Union Life Insurance Company
Fifth Third Bank
Fireman's Fund Insurance Companies
First Chicago Corporation
First Financial Group of New Hampshire,
Inc.
First Hawaiian Bank
First International Bancshares, Inc.
First Jersey National Bank
First & Merchants Corporation
First National Bank of Oregon
First National Bank of Southwestern
Michigan
First National Holding Corp.

First National Stores Inc.
First Pennsylvania Corporation
First Union Corporation
First Union, Incorporated
First United Bancorporation, Inc.
Firstmark Corporation
Fisher Scientific Company
Fleetwood Enterprises, Inc.
The Fleming Companies, Inc.
Florida Power Corporation
Florida Power & Light Company
Fluor Corporation
Foremost-McKesson, Inc.
Foster Wheeler Corporation
Fruehauf Corporation
Fuqua Industries, Inc.
GTI Corporation
Gannett Co., Inc.
The Garcia Corporation
Gardner-Denver Company
The Gas Service Company
General American Transportation
  Corporation
General Dynamics Corporation
General Electric Company
General Foods Corporation
General Mills, Inc.
General Motors Corporation
General Radio Company
General Refractories Company
General Reinsurance Corporation
General Signal Corporation
General Steel Industries, Inc.
General Telephone Company of California
General Telephone & Electronics
  Corporation
The General Tire & Rubber Company
Genesco, Inc.
Genuine Parts Company
Georgia Power Company
Gerber Products Company
Giddings & Lewis, Inc.
Gilbert Associates, Inc.
The Gillette Company
The Girard Company
Golden State Foods Corp.
The Goldfield Corporation
B. F. Goodrich Company
Government Employees Insurance Company
W. R. Grace & Co.
Graniteville Company
GranTree Corporation
The Great Atlantic & Pacific Tea Co., Inc.
Great Southwest Corporation
The Great-West Life Assurance Company
Great Western Financial Corporation

Green Giant Company
The Greyhound Corporation
Grumman Corporation
Gulf Oil Corporation
Gulf Resources & Chemical Corporation
Hackensack Water Company and
  Subsidiaries
Hamilton Allied Corporation
John Hancock Mutual Life Insurance
  Company
Handy & Harman
The Hanna Mining Company
Hannaford Bros. Co.
Harris Bankcorp, Inc.
Harsco Corporation
Hartford National Corp.
Hawaiian Electric Company, Inc.
Hayes-Albion Corporation
H. J. Heinz Company
Walter E. Heller International Corp.
Hemisphere Fund, Inc.
Hercules Incorporated
Hesston Corporation
Hewlett-Packard Company
Hexcel Corporation
The Higbee Company
Hillenbrand Industries, Inc.
Hilton Hotels Corporation
Hoerner Waldorf Corporation
Holly Sugar Corporation
The Horn & Hardart Company
Host International, Inc.
Houdaille Industries, Inc.
Household Finance Corporation
Houston Lighting & Power Company
Houston Oil & Minerals Corporation
Howmet Corporation
The Huffman Manufacturing Company
The E. F. Hutton Group Inc.
Huyck Corporation
Hyster Company
Idaho Power Co.
Ideal Basic Industries, Inc.
Ideal Toy Corporation
Illini Beef Packers, Inc.
Illinois Tool Works Inc.
Independent Bankshares Corporation
Indian Head Inc.
Indiana Gas Company, Inc.
Indianapolis Life Insurance Co.
Industrial Valley Bank and Trust Company
Industries Trend Fund, Inc.
Inexco Oil Company
Inland Container Corporation
Inland Steel Company
Inmont Corporation

Inspiration Consolidated Copper Company
Interco Incorporated
Interlake, Inc.
Intermountain Gas Company
International Business Machines
  Corporation
International Flavors & Fragrances, Inc.
International General Industries, Inc.
International Harvester Company
International Minerals & Chemical
  Corporation
International Paper Company
International Rectifier Corporation
Interpace Corporation
The Interpublic Group of Companies, Inc.
Iowa Beef Processors, Inc.
Iowa Electric Light and Power Company
Iowa Power and Light Company
Itek Corporation
Itel Corporation
Jantzen Inc.
Jewel Companies, Inc.
Johns-Manville Corporation
Johnson Controls, Inc.
Johnson & Johnson
Earle M. Jorgensen Co.
Kaiser Industries Corporation
Kaneb Services, Inc.
Kansas City Southern Industries, Inc.
Kansas-Nebraska Natural Gas Company,
  Inc.
Kearney & Trecker Corporation
Kellwood Company
Kelly Services, Inc.
Kentucky Utilities Company
Keuffel & Esser Company
Kewanee Oil Company
Keyes Fibre Company
Keystone Consolidated Industries, Inc.
Kimberly-Clark Corporation
King Radio Corp.
Kirsch Company
Koehring Company
Kollmorgen Corporation
Koppers Company, Inc.
Kraftco Corporation
S. S. Kresge Company
Kroehler Mfg. Co.
The Kroger Co.
W. A. Krueger Co.
Kuhlman Corporation
The LTV Corporation
La Salle National Bank
Laclede Steel Company
The Lamson & Sessions Co.
Latrobe Steel Company

Lehigh Portland Cement Company
Lenox, Incorporated
Leslie Salt Company
Libbey-Owens-Ford Company
Libby, McNeill & Libby
The Liberty Corporation
Liberty Loan Corporation
Liberty Mutual Insurance Company
Liberty National Life Insurance Company
Life Insurance Company of Georgia
Eli Lilly and Company
Lincoln First Banks Inc.
Lincoln National Corporation
The Lionel Corporation
Lipe-Rollway Corporation
Arthur D. Little, Inc.
Litton Industries, Inc.
Lodge & Shipley Co.
Lone Star Steel Company
Long Island Lighting Company
The Louisiana Land and Exploration
  Company
Louisville Gas and Electric Company
Louisville and Nashville Railroad Company
Lucky Stores, Inc.
Lukens Steel Company
Lykes-Youngstown Corporation
Lynch Communication Systems, Inc.
Lyon Metal Products, Incorporated
McCormick & Company, Incorporated
McDonnell Douglas Corporation
McDonough Company
McGraw-Edison Company
McGraw-Hill, Inc.
McQuay-Perfex Inc.
MBPXL Corporation
The Magnavox Company
Mallinckrodt, Inc.
P. R. Mallory & Co. Inc.
Manufacturers Hanover Trust Company
Manufacturers National Bank of Detroit
Marathon Oil Company
Marcor Inc.
Maremont Corporation
Marine Colloids, Inc.
The Marine Corporation
Marine Midland Banks, Inc.
Marriott Corporation
Marshall Field & Company
Maryland Cup Corporation
Maryland National Corporation
Masonite Corporation
Massachusetts Investors Trust
Massachusetts Mutual Life Insurance
  Company
The May Department Stores Company

Oscar Mayer & Co., Inc.
The Maytag Company
The Mead Corporation
Measurex Corp.
Medalist Industries, Inc.
Medenco, Inc.
Medusa Corporation
Menasco Manufacturing Company
Merrill Lynch & Co., Inc.
Metropolitan Life Insurance Company
Michigan Consolidated Gas Company
Michigan Gas Utilities Company
Michigan General Corporation
Michigan Mutual Insurance Company
Midland-Ross Corporation
Milgo Electronic Corporation
Minnesota Mining and Manufacturing
 Company
Mirro Aluminum Co.
Mississippi River Corporation
Missouri Pacific Railroad Company
Mitchell Energy & Development Corp.
The Mohawk Rubber Company
Monroe Auto Equipment Company
Monsanto Company
The Montana Power Company
Moore McCormack Resources, Inc.
Morrison-Knudsen Company, Inc.
Morse Shoe, Inc.
Morton-Norwich Products, Inc.
Motorola, Inc.
Mountain Fuel Supply Co.
Munford, Inc.
Murphy Oil Corporation
NCNB Corporation
NL Industries, Inc.
NLT Corporation
Nabisco, Inc.
Nalco Chemical Company
Nashua Corporation
National Can Corporation
National Homes Corporation
National Life Insurance Co.
National-Standard Company
National Utilities & Industries Corporation
Nationwide Corporation
Natomas Company
Neptune International Corporation
New England Electric System
New England Fish Company
New England Gas and Electric Association
New England Merchants Company, Inc.
New England Mutual Life Insurance
 Company
New York Life Insurance Company
New York State Electric & Gas Corporation

The New York Times Company
Niagara Mohawk Power Corporation
Nolex Corporation
Norlin Music Inc.
Norris Oil Co.
Northern Illinois Gas Company
Northern Natural Gas Company
Northern States Power Company
Northwest Bancorporation
Northwest Energy Company
Northwest Industries, Inc.
Northwest Natural Gas Company
Northwestern National Life Insurance
 Company
Northwestern Steel and Wire Company
Norton Company
Nortrust Corporation
Noxell Corporation
Occidental Life Insurance Co. of California
Occidental Petroleum Corporation
Oglebay Norton Company
The Ohio Brass Company
Ohio Edison Company
The Ohio River Company
Oklahoma Gas and Electric Company
Old Stone Corporation
Olin Corporation
Olincraft, Inc.
Olympia Brewing Company
The Omaha National Bank
Omark Industries, Inc.
Otis Elevator Company
Paccar Inc.
Pacific Gas and Electric Company
Pacific Holding Corporation
Pacific Resources, Inc.
Pacific Tin Consolidated Corporation
Paine Webber Incorporated
Pan Ocean Oil Corporation
Panhandle Eastern Pipe Line Company
Parker-Hannifin Corporation
The Parker Pen Company
Peachtree Doors, Inc.
J. C. Penney Company, Inc.
Pennwalt Corporation
Pennzoil Company
Peoples Gas Company
PepsiCo, Inc.
The Perkin-Elmer Corporation
Pertec Corporation
Pet Incorporated
Petrolane Incorporated
Petrolite Corporation
Phelps Dodge Corporation
Philadelphia Electric Company
Philadelphia Life Insurance Company

The Philadelphia National Bank
Philips Industries Inc.
Phoenix Mutual Life Insurance Company
The Pillsbury Company
Pioneer Corporation
Pitney-Bowes, Inc.
Planning Research Corporation
Polaroid Corporation
Portland General Electric Company
Potlatch Corporation
Premier Industrial Corporation
The Procter & Gamble Company
Provident Life and Accident Insurance
   Company
Public Service Company of Colorado
Public Service Company of Indiana
Public Service Company of New Hampshire
Public Service Company of New Mexico
Putnam Trust Company of Greenwich
Quaker Chemical Corporation
The Quaker Oats Company
Questor Corporation
RCA Corporation
The Rath Packing Company
Raybestos-Manhattan, Inc.
Raymond International Inc.
Recognition Equipment Incorporated
Reed Tool Company
Republic Steel Corporation
Research-Cottrell, Inc.
Revere Copper and Brass Incorporated
Revlon, Inc.
Rexham Corporation
Rexnord Inc.
R. J. Reynolds Industries, Inc.
Reynolds Metals Company
Richardson-Merrell Inc.
Richmond Corporation
Richmond, Fredericksburg and Potomac
   Railroad Co.
Riegel Textile Corporation
The Riggs National Bank of Washington,
   D.C.
Rio Grande Industries, Inc.
H. H. Robertson Co.
A. H. Robins Company, Incorporated
Rochester Gas and Electric Corporation
Rocket Research Corporation
Rockwell International Corporation
Rogers Corporation
Rohr Industries, Inc.
Rorer-Amchem, Inc.
Rowland, Incorporated
Royal Crown Cola Co.
Rubbermaid Incorporated
The Rucker Company

Ryder System, Inc.
S. W. Industries, Inc.
Safeguard Industries, Inc.
Safeway Stores, Incorporated
St. Joe Minerals Corporation
St. Joseph Light & Power Company
The St. Paul Companies, Inc.
San Diego Gas & Electric Company
Sanders Associates, Inc.
Santa Fe Industries, Inc.
Santa Fe International Corporation
Sargent-Welch Scientific Company
B. F. Saul Real Estate Investment Trust
Schering-Plough Corporation
Schick Incorporated
Schiller Industries, Inc.
Scholastic Magazines, Inc.
Scientific-Atlanta, Inc.
Scott, Foresman and Co.
Scott Paper Company
Scovill Manufacturing Company
Sea Pines Company
Seaboard Coast Line Industries, Inc.
Seaboard World Airlines
Sealed Power Corporation
G. D. Searle & Co.
Sears, Roebuck and Co.
Sentry Insurance & Mutual Company
Service Master Industries Inc.
Servomation Corporation
The Seven-Up Company
Shelter Resources Corporation
The Sherwin-Williams Company
Sierra Pacific Power Company
Signode Corporation
Simplicity Pattern Co. Inc.
A. O. Smith Corporation
SmithKline Corporation
Snap-On Tools Corporation
Society Corporation
Sorg Printing Company Incorporated
SOS Consolidated Inc.
South Carolina Electric & Gas Company
South Jersey Industries, Inc.
Southeast Banking Corporation
The Southern Company
Southern California Edison Company
Southern Pacific Company
Southern Railway Company
Southern Union Gas Company
The Southland Corporation
Southland Financial Corporation
Southwest Bancshares, Inc.
Southwestern Electric Power Company
Southwestern Electric Service Company
Southwestern Life Corporation

Springs Mills, Inc.
Squibb Corporation
Stanadyne, Inc.
Standard Oil Company of California
Standard Oil Company (Indiana)
The Standard Oil Company (Ohio)
Standex International Corporation
Stanley Home Products, Inc.
The Stanley Works
State Street Boston Financial Corporation
Stauffer Chemical Company
Sterling Drug, Inc.
Sterling Electronics Corporation
J. P. Stevens & Co., Inc.
Stewart-Warner Corporation
Stone & Webster, Incorporated
Sunbeam Corporation
Sundstrand Corporation
Sunset Life Insurance Company of America
Super Food Services, Inc.
Super Valu Stores, Inc.
Surety Financial Corporation
Sysco Corporation
Szabo Food Service, Inc.
Tampa Electric Company
Tandy Corporation
The Tappan Company
Technicolor, Inc.
Tektronix, Inc.
Teleflex Incorporated
Tenneco Inc.
Tenney Engineering, Inc.
Texaco Inc.
Texas American Bancshares Inc.
Texas Eastern Transmission Corporation
Texas Gas Transmission Corporation
Texas Instruments Incorporated
Texas Oil & Gas Corp.
Texas Utilities Company
The Texstar Corporation
Thomas & Betts Corporation
J. Walter Thompson Company
The TI Corporation (of California)
Tiger International, Inc.
Time Incorporated
The Times Mirror Company
Todd Shipyards Corporation
The Toledo Edison Company
Topps Chewing Gum, Inc.
The Trane Company
Trans World Airlines, Inc.
Transamerica Corporation
Transco Companies, Inc.
Trans Union Corporation
Transway International Corporation
The Travelers Insurance Corporation

Tri-Continental Corporation
Trust Company of Georgia
Tucson Gas & Electric Company
Twentieth Century-Fox Film Corporation
UAL, Inc.
UGI Corporation
URS Corporation
UV Industries, Inc.
Union Bank
Union Camp Corporation
Union Carbide Corporation
The Union Corporation
Union Oil Company of California
Union Pacific Corporation
Union Special Corporation
United Financial Corporation of California
United Gas Pipe Line Company
U.S. Bancorp
United States Filter Corporation
United States Gypsum Company
U.S. Leasing International, Inc.
USLife Corporation
U.S. Natural Resources, Inc.
United States Steel Corporation
United Technologies Corporation
United Telecommunications, Inc.
United Virginia Bankshares, Inc.
Universal Foods Corporation
Universal Oil Products Company
The Upjohn Company
Utah International Inc.
V. F. Corporation
VSI Corporation
Veeder Industries Inc.
Viacom International Inc.
Viking Industries, Inc.
Virginia Electric and Power Company
Vulcan Materials Company
The Wachovia Corporation
E. R. Wagner Manufacturing Company
Warnaco, Inc.
Warner-Lambert Company
Washington Gas Light Company
Washington National Corporation
Washington Natural Gas Company
The Washington Post Company
The Washington Water Power Company
Waste Management, Inc.
Wean United, Inc.
Wells Fargo Bank
West Point-Pepperell, Inc.
Westates Petroleum Company
Western Air Lines, Inc.
Western Electric Company, Inc.
Western Kentucky Gas Company
Western Publishing Company, Inc.

Western Union Corporation
Westinghouse Electric Corporation
Westvaco Corporation
Weyerhaeuser Company
Wheelabrator-Frye Inc.
Whirlpool Corporation
White Motor Corporation
Whittaker Corporation
The Wickes Corporation
The Williams Companies
Winn-Dixie Stores, Inc.

Winnebago Industries, Inc.
Wisconsin Electric Power Company
Witco Chemical Corporation
Dean Witter Organization Inc.
Woodward & Lothrop Incorporated
F. W. Woolworth Co.
Wm. E. Wright Co.
Xerox Corporation
The Youngstown Steel Door Company
Zenith Radio Corporation